Sharing Secrets

Sharing Secrets

Nineteenth-Century Women's Relations in the Short Story

Christine Palumbo-DeSimone

Madison • Teaneck
Fairleigh Dickinson University Press
London: Associated University Presses

Associated University Presses
440 Forsgate Drive
Cranbury, NJ 08512

Associated University Presses
16 Barter Street
London WC1A 2AH, England

Associated University Presses
P.O. Box 338, Port Credit
Mississauga, Ontario
Canada L5G 4L8

The paper used in this publication meets the requirements of the American National Standard for Permanence of Paper for Printed Library Materials Z39.48-1984.

Library of Congress Cataloging-in-Publication Data

Palumbo-DeSimone, Christine, 1964–
    Sharing Secrets : nineteenth-century women's relations in the short story / Christine Palumbo-DeSimone.
        p. cm.
    Includes bibliographical references (p.) and index.
    ISBN 0-8386-3840-6 (alk. paper)
        1. Short stories, American—Women authors—History and criticism.   2. Women and literature—United States—History—19th century.   3. Women and literature—Great Britain—History—19th century.   4. American fiction—19th century—History and criticism.   5. English fiction—Women authors—History and criticism.   6. English fiction—19th century—History and criticism.   7. Short stories, English—History and criticism.   8. Female friendship in literature.   I. Title.

PS374.W6 P35 2000
813'.0109352042—dc21

                                                                                                99-053350

PRINTED IN THE UNITED STATES OF AMERICA

For Frank, Mia, and Gianna

Contents

Acknowledgments

The Bonds of Womanhood: "Women's Sphere" in New England, 1780–1835, Nancy F. Cott. Reproduced with permission of Yale University Press, New Haven, CT.

"Separatism as Strategy: Female Institution Building and American Feminism, 1870–1930," Estelle Freedman. Reprinted from *Feminist Studies,* Volume 5:3 (Fall 1979) by permission of the publisher, *Feminist Studies,* Inc., College Park, MD.

"The Female World of Love and Ritual: Relations Between Women in Nineteenth-Century America," Carroll Smith-Rosenberg. Reprinted from *Signs,* Volume 1 (1975) by permission of the publisher, University of Chicago Press, Chicago, IL.

The Biosocial Construction of Femininity: Mothers and Daughters in Nineteenth-Century America, Nancy M. Theriot. Copyright (c) 1988 by Nancy M. Theriot. Reproduced with permission of Greenwood Publishing Group, Inc., Westport, CT.

Sharing Secrets

1

"Bold, Frank, and Truthful": "Great Books," Encoded Meanings and Nineteenth-Century Women's Short Stories

A great book is yet unwritten about women. Michelet has aired his waxdoll theories regarding them. The defender of "woman's rights" has given us her views. Authors and authoresses of little, and big repute, have expressed themselves on this subject, and none of them as yet have begun to grasp it: men—because they lack spirituality, rightly and justly to interpret women; women—because they dare not, or will not tell us that which most interests us to know. Who shall write this bold, frank, truthful book remains to be seen. Meanwhile, woman's millennium is yet a great way off . .
—Fanny Fern, "The Working Girls of New York"

IN SUSAN GLASPELL'S "A JURY OF HER PEERS" (1917), MARTHA HALE is abruptly pulled from her busy kitchen to accompany Mrs. Peters and a small group of men to the remote farm of John and Minnie Wright.[1] While the men explore the house for clues to substantiate what they believe has transpired—John Wright has been found strangled, and his wife Minnie is charged with murder—the two women are left to collect from among the kitchen things a few personal belongings for the accused. As Mrs. Hale surveys Minnie Foster's chaotic kitchen—"she still thought of her as Minnie Foster, though for twenty years she had been Mrs. Wright" (257)—she notices an uncovered wooden bucket of sugar and beside it a paper bag left only half full:

> Mrs. Hale moved toward it.
> "She was putting this in there," she said to herself—slowly.
> She thought of the flour in her kitchen at home—half sifted, half not sifted. She had been interrupted, and had left things half done. What had interrupted Minnie Foster? Why had that work been left half done? (266–67)

Of course, Mrs. Hale's questions put in motion the process of revelation that is the crux of Glaspell's story. Slowly, by placing together the "trifles" of Minnie Foster's kitchen (*Trifles* was the play version which Glaspell based on the same murder case), the two women get a picture of Minnie's hard and desperately lonely life with John Wright and come to understand how Wright's final act of cruelty—the strangling of Minnie's pet canary—proved the outrage that shattered Minnie's submissiveness and sanity. By looking at Minnie Foster's kitchen and asking "What happened here?" Mrs. Hale and Mrs. Peters are able to solve the "mystery" of Wright's murder and subsequently to become the "jury" that exonerates Minnie based on the story it constructs.

The men who are so diligently looking for "clues" never read this story, however. The central irony in "A Jury of Her Peers" lies in the men's smug self-assurance that, in fact, there is no "story" in Minnie Foster's kitchen at all. Although the sheriff and the county attorney search the rest of the house for evidence of a motive, they completely ignore the kitchen, regarding it as outside the realm of significant action:

> [The county attorney] paused and looked around the kitchen.
> "You're convinced there was nothing important here?" he asked the sheriff. "Nothing that would—point to any motive?"
> The sheriff too looked all around, as if to re-convince himself.
> "Nothing here but kitchen things," he said, with a little laugh for the insignificance of kitchen things. (263)

Indeed, this very confidence in "the insignificance of kitchen things" ultimately precludes the men's even asking the critical question, "What happened here?", since they are "convinced" (and any further examination serves only to "re-convince" them) that nothing of meaning *could* have happened in the kitchen. After all, the murder—the overt, real "act" in the story—occurred in the bedroom; what of importance could possibly have happened outside of such direct, observable action? In the two contrasting interpretations of Minnie Foster's kitchen, the fundamental distinction between the two women's "reading" and the men's "misreading" (or "missed-reading") lies not so much in what answers the parties come up with to explain the situation but in which questions are asked in the first place. Significantly, solving the mystery of John Wright's murder involves not merely asking "What happened?" at the scene of the crime, but also asking "What happened?" where it might at first seem that *nothing* has happened. In effect, the murder plot in Glaspell's story requires a rethinking of the notion of "action" to include apparent stillness.

"A Jury of Her Peers" is more than an ironic, insightful commentary on male-female relations and understanding; it is a useful starting point for considering how readers process "stories" in general and short stories in particular. Mrs. Hale's key question—"What happened here?"—is, in fact, asked of all mysteries (texts) which must be solved (read). However, the answer traditionally given regarding nineteenth-century women's stories has been that *nothing* happens or, more directly, that what takes place in nineteenth-century women's short fiction is so commonplace, inconsequential, "trifling," that it bears little true literary interest and significance. Fred Lewis Pattee's *The Development of the American Short Story* chiefly recognizes nineteenth-century women's stories in order to denigrate them, decrying the "orgy of feminine sentimentalism and emotionalism" that presumably characterized women's stories.[2] Even when Pattee is less scathing in his criticism, he is no less dismissive regarding such stories' relevance; while acknowledging that the work of many late-nineteenth-century New England women is "well done," Pattee concludes that it nevertheless "has added little that need detain the student of the American short story evolution."[3]

Admittedly, at first glance, many nineteenth-century women's stories do appear startlingly "uneventful" because little real "action" seems to take place: in Lydia Maria Child's "The Neighbour-In-Law" (1846), two women become friendly neighbors; in Susan Pettigru King Bowen's "A Marriage of Persuasion" (1857), a daughter is convinced to marry; in Sarah Orne Jewett's "Miss Tempy's Watchers" (1888), two women watch over a dead friend's body. But the broad critical assumption that such stories are inherently inconsequential parallels the men's conviction in Glaspell's story that "nothing important" transpired in Minnie Foster's kitchen; it keeps readers from subsequently asking what should be an array of logical questions about women's "uneventful" stories: *Why* are many women's stories framed around seemingly meaningless incidents? *Why* do they lack any overtly discernible action? *Why*, to use Glaspell's story again, do we not see the "real," sensational action of the murder, but instead see the kitchen of the accused? If women's stories, like the work in

Minnie Foster's kitchen, at times seem "half done," then the reader's next step should be to follow Mrs. Hale's lead and wonder why things have been left so.

These questions call not only for a reconsideration of the content of nineteenth-century women's stories (itself an important endeavor) but also for an analysis of the stories' structures. It is tempting in the context of Poe's macabre murders, O. Henry's "snapper" endings, and Melville's sea adventures to accept Pattee's verdict that nineteenth-century women's short stories are often inscrutable simply because they are not good and to dismiss women's stories as somehow outside the "mainstream" of American short fiction. But the very context of nineteenth-century short story production itself prohibits the disregard Pattee and others have shown for women's stories. Hawthorne's famous 1854 tirade against the "damn'd mob of scribbling women" who presumably were ruining his own chances for success points to (among other things) the irrefutable fact that women's fiction *sold* and that nineteenth-century readers—in unprecedented numbers—were willing to pay the subscription price for countless magazines featuring women's short stories. While Hawthorne and others reviled women's writing, clearly there was a vast audience for such stories, and by and large that audience was female. Cathy N. Davidson notes that the woman reader was also the "implied reader" of most popular fiction throughout the Revolutionary Era, making an indelible impression on the forms and functions of the emerging American novel.[4] And Nancy Woloch, in *Women and the American Experience,* explains how literacy and prosperity created a large middle-class female market for fiction in nineteenth-century America, noting that by the 1850s women comprised an estimated four-fifths of the popular reading public.[5] Thus, instead of dismissing woman's stories as "add[ing] little that need detain the student of the American short story," we should instead pose two more questions: Why were women's stories so enormously popular in the nineteenth century? And why, until quite recently in literary scholarship, have such widely read women's stories been largely overlooked?

The growing list of questions already posed indicates how little we truly know about many nineteenth-century women's short stories. Surely part of the reason why such stories frequently seem "strange" to today's readers is a basic unfamiliarity with the works. Pattee's advice to "the student of the American short story," to ignore the huge body of nineteenth-century women's short fiction, echoes the dominant sentiment of literary criticism for decades. A brief look at the table of contents in a work such as Arthur Voss's *The American Short Story: A Critical Survey* reveals the critical ghettoization of nineteenth-century women's stories; chapter 1 is titled "The Beginnings of the American Short Story: Washington Irving," and successive chapters are dedicated to Hawthorne and Melville, Poe, Bret Hart, and Mark Twain. Women receive no attention until chapter five, and then as merely among the "others" who wrote "regional stories."[6] Voss's categorization of women's stories as primarily extraneous to the main current of American short fiction is by no means extraordinary, and I could well have cited a dozen like studies which handle women's stories in a similar fashion. In commenting on the "critical invisibility" of countless widely read women writers, Nina Baym asks, "How is it possible for a critic or historian of American literature to leave these books, and these authors, out of the picture?"[7] The fact that feminist scholars over the last twenty or so years have needed to "rediscover" women's short stories points to how new our inquiries into these works are and how much must be done to understand them fully.

Ironically, however, it might well be argued that some of the very "rediscovery" projects that have retrieved women's stores from literary obscurity have done little to make them accessible to readers. In working to reclaim a female short-story tradition, some feminist scholars have been startlingly uncritical in their assessment of women's tales and have failed to address the structural considerations that might have illuminated women's texts. For example, in her Introduction to *Women Writers of the Short Story: A Collection of Critical Essays,* Heather McClave writes,

> the importance of many of these scribbling women has little to do with art but much to do with history. Accustomed as we are now to a more egalitarian climate, we forget too easily that in the 1850s women can not yet go to college, or speak freely in public, or choose a profession, or vote in general elections . . . yet they write in large numbers, using their own names, recording their own experiences. They show under pressure that women *can* write, not only as exceptional geniuses but also as commercially successful hacks. Thus they open the field for a new tradition.[8]

But the premise that nineteenth-century women's stories are important not as "art" but as "history" overlooks the fact that women's stories were *produced* as art (whether "genius" or "hack"), and ultimately leads to a reductive argument that women's texts are noteworthy solely because they were written by women. With such an approach, women's stories simply are as they are, and the reasons behind their often puzzling design remain obscure. To use again Glaspell's story as a metaphor for critical analysis, many early rediscovery projects resist the notion that only "trifles" can be found in Minnie Foster's kitchen and deliberately take the time to survey Minnie's world. However, such criticism does not really scrutinize the disarray it sometimes finds; it does not question why the kitchen has been left so and what its arrangement might mean. Surely Minnie's kitchen has significance beyond its being a kitchen?

A second approach to nineteenth-century women's stories that at times has proven limited in analyzing structure has been the effort to "redeem" these peculiar stories by focusing on how the texts fit into twentieth-century feminist paradigms. Surely feminist scholarship has provided vital tools for finding meaning in nineteenth-century women's stories, as the feminist readings of Glaspell's "A Jury of Her Peers" reveal. But the problem with reading primarily for what nineteenth-century women's stories say to "us" is that it still does not account for the tremendous appeal of women's stories *in the nineteenth century*. In *Revolution and the Word*, Cathy N. Davidson states,

> It is simply too easy to perpetuate assumptions about the reader that neglect the inescapable fact that readers, as much as texts, operate within historical contexts. Having wisely revalued authors and texts, contemporary criticism still perpetuates its worst tendencies when it attempts to valorize an ostensibly historical reader who turns out to be mostly another apotheosis of the contemporary literary theorist.[9]

Discovering feminist themes in nineteenth-century women's stories is, of course, quite rewarding to feminist critics, but can we legitimately assume that our pleasure parallels that of a nineteenth-century reader? As Susan K. Harris points out in her analysis of nineteenth-century women's novels, in re-evaluating nineteenth-century women's works we must be ever mindful of "functional and historical" considerations, and ask, "What needs did [women's texts] serve for their intended audience?"[10] Feminist scholarship of the last two decades has convincingly demonstrated the inadequacy of canonical standards for reading women's texts since, as Annette Kolodny states, reading constitutes "interpretive strategies that are learned, historically determined, and thereby necessarily gender-inflected."[11] Likewise, the critical pretense that the "reading" performed by twentieth-century feminist academia can match that of a nineteenth-century popular female audience is equally false and reductive. In this light, Harris calls for a "process" approach to reading nineteenth-century women's literature, "to see it within the shifting currents of nineteenth-century American ideologies."[12] Such observations reveal that Fanny Fern's 1868 belief that the "great book" about women remains "unwritten" is not entirely true; such a "book" about nineteenth-century women's lives has indeed been written, but we have yet to learn to read it.

Still another obstacle in our road to understanding the sometimes puzzling stories of nineteenth-century women lies in the very fact that they are short stories and thus belong to a somewhat "problematic" genre in American literature. From Edgar Allan Poe's "Review of the Twice-Told Tales" (1842) to the present, critics have long debated not merely how to write or read the short story, but how to define the form itself. Brander Matthews defined the short story through its unique effect on the reader; Mary Rohrberger rejected the focus on "effect" to define the short story in terms of its "overall purpose and structure"; H. E. Bates asserted that the short story's "infinite flexibility" gives rise to a genre that has never been adequately defined.[13] Discussions of the short story invariably include how the story compares to the novel which is (whether intentionally or not) set up as the narrative and cultural norm against which the short story must be assessed and defended. The critical impulse to define the American short story through its relationship to a more dominant literary form is quite telling. Clare Hanson keenly notes how the huge commercial success of women's stories in weekly magazines "has undoubtedly helped to fix the form as popular and/or inferior in the minds of literary criticism" and has kept the short story "ex-centric" in terms of official cultural hegemony.[14] But the debate over how to define the short story also reveals the complexity of discerning how the short story actually "works" and the tremendous difficulty of determining precisely where the genre's appeal really lies. Thus, in attempting to explain the vast popularity of nineteenth-century women's stories with their contemporary audience, we must take into account the dual nature of such works as both women's stories and as short stories.

The short story is, of course, "short"; hence, by definition, it is limited in its scope regardless of how a particular writer or editor might

interpret the term. The genre therefore calls for a limited cast of
characters to be presented, a limited number of scenes to be staged,
a limited array of emotions to be displayed or elicited. In essence, the
genre renders a limited reality. The short story, however, cannot be
defined solely through its limitations, for each work must also meet
the genre's other criterion of being, in some sense, a "story." In this
respect, Poe's "unity of effect,"[15] while far from exhaustive, offers
both a starting point for considering the appeal of the short story
genre and a nineteenth-century critical context. In lauding the prose
tale as "the fairest field for the exercise of the loftiest talent"[16] that
can be realized in prose, Poe points specifically to the sense of "totality"[17] the reader experiences with the short story. While, for Poe,
such "totality" is chiefly derived from the genre's brevity (the story's
capacity to be "completed at one sitting"),[18] his comments nevertheless indicate a key structural consideration in determining how the
form works. Though "short," the short story must nonetheless instill
in its reader a sense that the "story" has been told, a feeling that the
reality—albeit limited—has been played out. The short story reader
achieves satisfaction for her efforts through the genre's relatively
quick return of a tale that is essentially "complete." As Heather Mc-
Clave observes, "The short story, like the lyric poem, embodies the
completed moment: immediate, self-contained, isolated from causal
chains of events."[19] Without this "completeness," readers perceive, as
do the men in Glaspell's story, that some integral piece of the puzzle
is "missing," and like the men they too are left "not satisfied" (280)
with what they have found.

   Here reader-response criticism proves a useful tool in tapping
into the short story's power. Wolfgang Iser has noted how all texts
contain "gaps," spaces where the text fails to relate directly important
information. Iser, however, contends that these "gaps" are themselves
significant, because they actually "give rise to communication [be-
tween text and reader] in the reading process":[20]

> What is missing . . . stimulates the reader into filling the blanks with pro-
> jections. He is drawn into the events and made to supply what is meant
> from what is not said. What is said only appears to take on significance as
> a reference to what is not said; it is the implications and not the statements
> that give shape and weight to the meaning. But as the unsaid comes to life
> in the reader's imagination, so the said "expands" to take on greater sig-
> nificance than might have been supposed: even trivial scenes can seem
> surprisingly profound.[21]

The dynamic between the "said" and the "unsaid" in the formation of meaning gains even greater authority in the short story, where structural measures to achieve brevity often require so much to be left "missing" from the written text. Clare Hanson suggests that the short story's limited scope be viewed not as a restriction but as a "frame" that assists the reader in interpreting the fragmented picture enclosed:

> The frame acts as an aesthetic device, permitting ellipses (gaps and absences) to remain in a story, which retains a necessary air of completeness and order because of the very existence of the frame.[22]

For the short story to "work," then, a pact is struck between the text and reader. On the one hand, the reader approaches the short story *knowing* that only part of the story will be "told," that the reader must supply the story's missing pieces. On the other, the "said" text itself must act as the clue to what is "unsaid," so that the reader *can,* in fact, "fill in the blanks," supply the unsaid, and achieve a "completed" tale.

The key, of course, is in recognizing the "clues," since, if they are missed, the "unity of effect"—the sense that a whole story has been realized within a limited reality—is lost. But, as "A Jury of Her Peers" illustrates, not all readers construct the "unsaid" in the same way. Stanley Fish contends that the interpretive strategies readers employ in creating the unsaid text are "not natural or universal, but learned."[23] Accordingly, readers who learn similar strategies (Fish's "interpretive communities")[24] will decipher a text's clues and fill in its blanks, based on their shared knowledge and experiences. The unsaid, then, becomes as much a social as a literary construct, since, ultimately, it represents a specific version of reality formed through cultural experience.

As Patrocinio P. Schweickart astutely notes in "Reading Ourselves," Fish's theories never take into account the enormous impact of gender on reader experience, an oversight that speaks volumes about the marginalized status of many women's works.[25] In reading, as Annette Kolodny asserts, "what we engage are not texts but paradigms," and such modes of understanding (like all learned behavior) are inescapably gendered.[26] Thus, the answer both to why nineteenth-century women's stories were so popular with their largely female audience and why those same stories have been neglected in predominantly male literary scholarship lies in the gendered nature of reading itself. "For simply put," Kolodny states, "we read well, and

with pleasure, what we already know how to read."[27] Kolodny's remarks suggest not only that nineteenth-century women's lives provided the means through which women could "read well and with
pleasure" other women's stories, but also reveal how the male-generated paradigms traditionally used to approach (and then dismiss)
nineteenth-century women's stories have prevented scholars from
reading such stories "well." Introducing gender into a reader-response approach to the short story brings to light where the work
must now be done in evaluating nineteenth-century women's stories,
for it shows how a rereading of women's stories will indeed "write"
the "great book" on women that Fanny Fern sought.

Specifically, our rereading of nineteenth-century women's short
stories must examine not just the unique content of women's "said"
texts but the forms and functions of the "unsaid" as well, since the
gaps that play such a vital role in short story structure are themselves
gendered constructs. A writer structures her "said" text so that her
reader will be able to comprehend the "unsaid" text, leaving unsaid
only what she assumes the reader will quickly and easily comprehend.
Hence, the writer decides what is told and what is left "understood"
based on her *own* knowledge and experience. It stands to reason that
nineteenth-century women's short stories will reflect a woman's
world not just in their subject matter but in their structure, since
women's distinct social experience ultimately underlies how the story
itself gets told. It is profoundly significant in Glaspell's "A Jury of Her
Peers" that Minnie Foster's sad story is never "told" but her plight is
instead expressed through the clues in her kitchen; the "unsaid" story
in "A Jury of Her Peers" exists only for those who can decipher Minnie's encoded cries of outrage and despair. In discovering Minnie's
desperate act, Mrs. Hale comments on the shared experience which
makes such understanding possible:

> I might 'a' *known* she needed help! I tell you, it's *queer,* Mrs. Peters. We
> live close together and we live far apart. We all go through the same
> things—it's all just a different kind of the same thing! If it weren't—why
> do you and I *understand?* Why do we *know*—what we know this minute?
> (279; emphasis Glaspell's)

"A Jury of Her Peers" is an example of how nineteenth-century
women writers used women's shared social experience as an *encoding
device,* a structural mechanism through which the unsaid story of Min-

nie Foster's life is both conveyed and understood. The fact that the men do not share in women's experience means that the clues in Minnie's kitchen not only fail to "speak" to them but that, in a fundamental way, the clues do not exist for the men. In an ironic attempt at being witty, Mr. Hale muses whether "the women [would] know a clue if they did come upon it" (266). By the end of the tale, however, it is the men who are "clueless," who are still searching for "Something to make a *story* about" (279; emphasis added).

As has been noted, the short story succeeds only when such a "story" materializes, when the reader's understanding of both the said and unsaid texts renders a completed tale. The "story" of nineteenth-century women's lives is thus most readily accessible and most fully comprehended by the female readers who shared the gendered experiences at the heart of women's tales and who could read the stories' "gaps" in such a way that the said story made sense. In writing to a primarily female popular audience, women writers structured their stories based on what they assumed *other women* would understand. Kolodny notes that the women in "A Jury of Her Peers" come to "recognize the profoundly sex-linked world of meaning which they inhabit"[28] and to see that they "know" another woman's life because, as Mrs. Hale states, "we all go through the same things." A parallel recognition of the "profoundly sex-linked" nature of reading will prove the means through which readers today may enter the closed, "secret" world of nineteenth-century women's short stories and may come to appreciate these stories' tremendous appeal for a nineteenth-century female audience.

Of course, had the two women in "A Jury of Her Peers" simply pointed out to the men the various pieces of evidence they had uncovered (Minnie's "crazy sewing" of a quilt patch, her half-done work, the strangled canary) and explained for them the significance of such "trifles," the men might well have been convinced that the farmwomen had found the motive so urgently needed. But the very fact that these details do not speak directly and immediately to the men in Glaspell's tale—that the "unsaid" story would have to be "said" in order to be constructed—indicates two important factors in considering nineteenth-century women's stories. First, the need to make explicit for an "outsider" that which is implicit for an informed reader unavoidably interrupts the immediacy of the short story's appeal, since the reader is unable to experience a "completed" tale from her own rendering of the unsaid.

Secondly, and perhaps more significantly, the need to explain the unsaid to "outsiders" makes it questionable whether such readers can ever construct the *same* story that the intended audience created. The men in Glaspell's story are looking for a motive, "some definite thing" (279) that will substantiate their version of events; it is doubtful that they would take the information the women could supply and use it to exonerate Minnie Foster, as the women do. Kolodny writes that "A Jury of Her Peers" is a clear example of how the male reader "is a *different kind* of reader" than a female reader, and that "where women are concerned, he is often an inadequate reader."[29] The inability of most predominantly-male literary scholarship to read adequately the "unsaid" stories in women's short fiction has undoubtedly contributed to the "critical invisibility"[30] of many nineteenth-century women's tales.

To be sure, the gendered quality of short-story encoding "works both ways," in that male writers use their gendered experience in structuring their texts and assume that their audience will read a story's "gaps" in much the same manner that they do. But, because the unsaid in men's short stories encodes an implicitly male reality, male-dominated literary criticism has tended to overlook the gender-inflected nature of men's texts and to attach the tag of "universality" to that which speaks to male readers. In "What Makes a 'Great' Short Story Great?" Thomas A. Gullason—like so many critics before him—points to the "timely and timeless"[31] quality of "great" short stories such as Chekhov's "The Lady with the Dog" and Hemingway's "Big Two-Hearted River," claiming that the very "staying power" of these texts is itself a criterion for "greatness."[32]

The circular logic of the "timeless" argument ("The works that we read must be great because we read them") is obvious; more telling, however, are Gullason's distinctions between "universal" short stories and "popular" stories. The popular short-story writer can only produce "one-dimensional, static, predictable, and transitory" texts, since he always writes "with an eye on his audience." Gullason concludes:

> Even though he may always have a small audience, the great short-story writer, with his great short story—and not the popular writer, with his popular story—keeps the form alive, brings it prestige, and makes it a worthy competitor with the other arts.[33]

Gullason's fable of the writer who writes without a context—with no "eye" whatsoever to the identity of his reader—reveals the extent to which Gullason takes for granted the "sameness" between the "great" short-story writer and the discerning reader. This elite coterie of "knowing" readers bestows "prestige" and "universality" on a story, regardless of whether it has a broad ("popular") appeal. In her *Feminist Theory, Women's Writing,* Laurie A. Finke states:

> . . . [I]t is a "fact" of cultural hegemony, part of the logic of marginalization, that whatever group is constructed as the "other" . . . will always be perceived as writing about less universal themes than those of the culturally dominant group. This criterion is characteristically evoked as an aesthetic ideal which can then be used to deny marginal groups representation in the canon.[34]

That both the "popular" writer and reader have long been female in American short-story history underscores the true distinction Gullason is making: the "universal" short story is "fresh, alive, and immediate"[35] to *male* readers and is thus deemed "great." Stories that do not appeal to this "small audience" can never achieve "immortality."[36]

Since men's and women's texts are unavoidably gendered, it would seem to follow that men's stories are as inaccessible to women readers as women's tales often prove to men, and that women too are the "different" and "inadequate" readers Kolodny describes. This is not wholly the case, however. Of course, women do not live men's lives, and the distinctions between male and female reality do render a woman a "different" reader from her male counterpart. But the dominant literary and cultural assumptions underlying remarks such as Gullason's, that male reality is the norm and that male experience constitutes the "universal," have compelled many women to become familiar with men's codes in a way men have not needed to reciprocate. In criticizing the gender bias of Stanley Fish's "interpretive communities," Schweickart writes,

> . . . unlike Fish, the feminist reader is also aware that the ruling interpretive communities are androcentric, and that this androcentricity is deeply etched in the strategies and modes of thought that have been introjected by all readers, women as well as men.[37]

That women have been trained to read men's texts, while men have not been taught to read women's, does not mean that women are entirely exempt from being the "inadequate readers" Kolodny cites. It does reveal, however, that men and women are "inadequate" readers of each other's stories in fundamentally different ways and that the difference has much to do with the relative social position of each group. In *Toward a New Psychology of Women,* Jean Baker Miller speaks to the pervasive influence of social power in the communication between dominant and subordinate groups and to how subordinate groups are compelled to express their difference and defiance in a language the dominants cannot understand: "Put simply, subordinates won't tell. . . . Subordinates, then, know much more about the dominants than vice versa."[38] Whereas men writers do not produce their texts with an "eye" to women readers, many women have nevertheless learned to recognize and value some of the "unsaid" clues provided by male-generated stories. To call again on Glaspell's story, Mrs. Peters and Mrs. Hale, in fact, *do* "know a clue" when they come upon it, and they know the story that the men will derive from such clues even though their own story about Minnie's life is much different.

Women have learned (even if "inadequately") to see the encoded meanings in men's short stories, but only recently have they begun to challenge why men's encoding devices are almost exclusively granted aesthetic worth. For example, G. R. Thompson, in lauding Poe's short fiction, notes that part of the pleasure on reading Poe lies in detecting how each story is "a tale within a tale within a tale."[39] Thompson suggests that a tale's "meaning" lies in the relationship between the various implied stories and their frames, rather than in the surface story offered by the dramatically involved narrator. For Thompson, the "unsaid" in a Poe tale exists within the ironic interplay between various levels of storytelling, and the reader senses the story's "completeness" when he senses incongruity—when he detects the irony of Montresor's revenge "with impunity" and recognizes the inconsistencies in his story.[40]

In many nineteenth-century women's short stories, however, "completeness" is realized not in seeing incongruity but in sensing the story's underlying consistency. As will be more fully shown in chapter 2, Mary E. Wilkins Freeman's "On the Walpole Road" (1884) is also "a tale within a tale within a tale," but in Freeman's story, the various levels of storytelling *complement* each other, and the reader attains a sense of "completeness" by detecting not tension but agreement between the multiple framed tales. Fred Pattee's advice to the inquiring "student of the American short story" has been to ignore a story such as Freeman's or to deem it an interesting, but ultimately insignificant, aberration in the main current of short story development. But in considering the different structures men and women often employ to tell a tale, Laurie Finke asks instead why one type of storytelling is privileged over another: "Why, to cite only one example, are irony and complexity valued over sentimentality and simplicity?" Fiske calls on feminist readers to "interrogate the process through which such values are produced, given authority, and disseminated within a particular historical and social formation."[41] In challenging the criteria on which canonical "inclusion" and "exclusion" are based, feminist criticism has shown that the traditional literary canon both defines aesthetic "worth" and expresses ideological agreement; in essence, to be included is to be "understood."

A recognition that "worth" is inextricably tied to "belonging" underlies the present study of women's short stories. I aim to show that many overtly "simple" nineteenth-century women's tales actually are just as richly detailed, deeply meaningful, and artistically intricate as are many of the time-honored pieces of the nineteenth-century, short story tradition. In this sense, my work will assert that such women's stories "belong" in the canon of celebrated and studied American stories.

My method of achieving this end will be to explore a somewhat different notion of "belonging," one that focuses on how women's stories "belonged" to their social and literary context and were thus a reflection and outgrowth of a unique nineteenth-century female experience. Historians such as Nancy Cott and Carroll Smith-Rosenberg have done much to provide a picture of "woman's sphere" in nineteenth-century America and to structure a method of approaching nineteenth-century female existence.[42] Similarly, critics such as Kolodny, Sandra M. Gilbert, and Susan Gubar have worked to reconstruct the "separate" literary sphere of nineteenth-century women's art; for, as Kolodny observes,

> . . . again and again, each woman who took up the pen [in the nineteenth century] had to confront anew her bleak premonition that, both as writers and as readers, women too easily became isolated islands of symbolic significance, available only to, and decipherable only by, one another.[43]

In discussing the means by which feminist scholars must break the "vicious circle" of "androcentric interpretive strategies" canonizing "androcentric texts," Schweickart calls for "the development of the reading strategies consonant with the concerns, experiences, and formal devices" that are unique to women's texts.[44] Discussing "narratives of community," Sandra A. Zagarell suggests that the unchallenged expectation of linear progression in a story has not only slighted women's texts but has at times created reductive and arbitrary categories for defining fiction:

> Given such expectations, fiction about modes of life that are collective, continuous, and undramatic . . . are puzzling; generally . . . readers either assume that the work has no story, often delegating it to the supposedly inferior category of the sketch, or impose familiar but inappropriate notions of linear plotting on it.[45]

By redefining dramatic action within a nineteenth-century female context, my work aims to show that "sketches" are as much "stories" as are more readily recognizable (and, hence, more formally "acceptable") literary forms. Only by considering fully the implications of writing and reading within nineteenth-century women's worlds can we begin to answer some of the questions first posed in this discussion, to read the "clues" and find the "motives" in nineteenth-century women's "secret" tales.

The two women in "A Jury of Her Peers" are able to see "what [Minnie's] kitchen had meant through all the years" (277) because, in fact, they are *already* Minnie's "peers" and have—as Mrs. Hale so aptly states—gone "through the same things" (279). Had they not, Glaspell's story suggests, the women's reading of Minnie Foster's kitchen might well have proven just as "inadequate" as was the men's.

Similarly, the question of what makes certain women "peers" and what constitutes "belonging" surfaced as a defining factor in my own work. When I first approached this project, I had hoped to undertake a much broader investigation of nineteenth-century women's stories than is represented in the final analysis. I eventually realized, however, that the encoding devices in short fiction are not simply gender-inflected, but frequently race- and class-inflected as well. In studying nineteenth-century American women, the critical impulse is at times too quick to paint the woman's world in sweeping strokes and create a scene where all women "belonged" to the "cult of true womanhood" so celebrated in scholarship. Such an image of women's experience, however, ignores the fact that "separate spheres" was essentially a social construct, "a metaphor for complex relations in social and economic contexts."[46] A more discerning scrutiny of nineteenth-century women's lives reveals how social factors generated women's differences as well as "sameness." Sara M. Evans, for example, discusses the social and economic pressures which excluded many nineteenth-century urban working-class women from the "separate spheres" paradigm:

> For working-class women the separation of the home and the world had little practical meaning. . . . Most working-class women paid little heed to the canon of domesticity. It fit too little of their reality to prompt any desire for emulation or conformity to its tenets.[47]

Similarly, as Elizabeth Fox-Genovese and Catherine Clinton have shown, African-American women played an entirely different (indeed, antithetical) role in the patriarchy than did their white counterparts, and both black womanhood and black experience were defined through such women's relative social positions.[48] Native American women and many immigrant women typically were excluded from the "true woman" model, and were commonly cast as the "other" against which nineteenth-century white middle-class women were contrasted. Since my approach to women's stories maintains that social experience affects a story's structure, it became increasingly clear that my study could not gloss over such differences without collapsing all women into some generic definition of nineteenth-century womanhood into which *no* group of women could rightly fit.

I therefore decided to focus the greater part of my study on the works of white, middle-class, native-born American women. The reasons for giving my work such a decidedly "traditional" (perhaps even "conservative") spin are in part tied to the very forces that render its scope somewhat "conventional." First, nineteenth-century middle-class women's short stories represent a huge body of writing, the sheer proportions of which warrant an investigation into common structural issues and devices. Second, at present, scholarship has recreated a much clearer picture of nineteenth-century middle-class female social reality than it has of many "other" women's lives. Certainly the pervasive interest in white women's domestic sphere reflects, at least on some level, the cultural biases of scholars themselves. Nonetheless, it also is undeniable that there exists much more written evidence of middle-class white women's private lives (in the form of extant diaries and correspondence) through which to reconstruct middle-class women's world than is available for the lives of working-class and minority women. A corollary to the assertion that women used their common experiences to convey meaning in short fiction is that the better we understand particular women and their world, the more fully we can read their works. At present, scholars, quite simply, know more about white middle-class women's private experience than they do about many other women's daily interactions.

The third rationale for limiting much of my discussion to white middle-class women's short stories is, at least in my eyes, the most significant with regard to the present study's place in the ongoing feminist re-visioning of the nineteenth-century American short story canon. In the current academic/political drive to "open up" the traditional literary canon, the works of white, native-born, middle-class women—writers such as Kate Chopin, Mary E. Wilkins Freeman, Charlotte Perkins Gilman, and Sarah Orne Jewett—have most often been introduced to "represent" nineteenth-century women's short fiction. As such, *these* texts stand the strongest chance of being adopted into any new canon of American literature and, consequently, of taking on at least some of the "universality" that canonization has traditionally bestowed on "accepted" works. Again, the preference for white middle-class women's stories over the works of "other" women reveals the cultural assumptions and priorities lurking in all scholarship, particularly scholarship aimed at defining (or redefining) what it means to "belong."

My present effort, however, to examine women's stories decidedly within their specific cultural context, works to draw attention to pervasive critical biases by emphasizing how white middle-class women's stories are fundamentally (both in content and in structure) white middle-class women's stories. Exploring how a particular group of women (in this case, middle-class whites) utilizes its unique experiences as a means to relate meaning in fiction *resists* the impulse to ignore the sometimes subtle racial and class differences in encoding devices, an oversight which inevitably works to negate "other" experiences. Throughout this book, I do refer periodically to stories by African-American, working-class, and native American women which seemed worthwhile comparisons to white women's texts in terms of short story structure and encoding. I feel I have been careful in such instances not to overstep the bounds of my own purpose by overstating the similarities of these stories to white women's texts, instead suggesting avenues for the further exploration of the works. I therefore am confident that the very rationale for limiting much of my work's focus will equally bring to light the need to read more critically the lives and works of *all* nineteenth-century women.

ing reader who sees and appreciates its somewhat evasive clues. The "real" story in "A Jury of Her Peers" is not in what "verdict" the women reach but in how the "jury" itself is formed. The bonding that takes place between the women—in the two farmwomen's realization that they are no different from Minnie, as well as in their tacit agreement as to what finally to do with the clues they find—is the true "action" in Glaspell's story. The means by which the women's bonding is achieved are largely implied; a knowing look between Mrs. Hale and Mrs. Peters is often all the reader sees of the women's mutual understanding. Yet, without a full appreciation of how Mrs. Hale, Mrs. Peters, and Minnie Foster become "peers," the "verdict" the women reach cannot really make sense. Mrs. Hale and Mrs. Peters do no simply pity Minnie; such a reading of their actions is both simplistic and patronizing. Instead, they realize that if Minnie is "guilty" then so are *they*, since their failure to maintain human ties with their isolated neighbor has contributed directly to Minnie's fall. Without this second "unsaid" women's relationship story, Glaspell's tale does not entirely "work," since a critical motive for female action (the very thing which proves so elusive to the men in the story) remains obscure. The "unity of effect" in "A Jury of Her Peers" is fully achieved only through women's relationships.

I have chosen to examine first the primary female relationship in nineteenth-century woman's sphere, the mother-daughter bond, and to explore how the mother-daughter experience structures many nineteenth-century women's stories. The next analysis of female-friendship stories is more an extension of the mother-daughter chapter than a marked break from it, since in many ways the intimate friendships that so enriched nineteenth-century women's lives and stories were deeply influenced by mother-daughter sentiments and priorities. In a similar fashion, the female-friendship issues discussed in chapter 3 have relevance to the subsequent analysis of the nineteenth-century women's "community" and the community stories in chapter 4. Thus I hope to reflect in the structure of my own work the fundamental role of "relatedness" in nineteenth-century middle-class women's lives and its pervasive influence on women's works by presenting not wholly distinct categories of relationship stories but more a continuum of female relationship themes and devices. In addition, by looking at women's stories as reflections of female "connectedness," I hope to underscore the complex integrity of nineteenth-century woman's sphere, thereby calling into question again critical assessments of these stories that disregard the nuances of the nine-teenth-century female world.

Significantly, Glaspell's "A Jury of Her Peers" closes with a con-spiracy of silence:

> Slowly, unwillingly, Mrs. Peters turned her head until her eyes met the eyes of the other woman. There was a moment when they held each other in a steady, burning look in which there was no evasion nor flinching. . . . For a moment Mrs. Peters did not move. And then she did it. (280)

Without ever voicing their "verdict," Mrs. Hale and Mrs. Peters de-cide to conceal the strangled canary and not relate the real story of Minnie Foster's kitchen. The two farmwomen never commit an out-right falsehood; their deception lies not in what is said but in what re-mains unsaid and in the women's assurance as to how the men will interpret their silence. In a similar fashion, nineteenth-century women's stories have largely stood in cryptic silence before literary judges. Conventional assumptions about what is meaningful—what "speaks"—have rendered scholars incapable of truly hearing the re-lationship stories that women tell. By listening for the cadences of women's intimacies in nineteenth-century women's short stories, readers become attuned to the subtle tones of female communica-tion and hear the stories *inside* the silence. In deciphering women's "secret" codes, we are finally granted access to the otherwise closed experience of the nineteenth-century "woman's sphere."

Fanny Fern believed that the "great book" of women's lives was yet "unwritten" because its legitimate authors "dare not or will not tell us that which most interests us to know." But as has been suggested, nineteenth-century middle-class women did indeed "dare" to tell their story; the "greatness" of their tale resides in the fact that such women told their story in their own way. Seeing women's texts with what Adrienne Rich calls "fresh eyes"[54] allows us to ground nine-teenth-century women's writing in a female-centered context and to generate readings of women's lives and works that are substantive, in-sightful, "complete." In this regard, the "bold, frank, truthful" story of nineteenth-century women which Fern so desired may cease to ap-pear "unwritten," and "woman's millennium" may no longer seem such "a great way off."

2

"Family Secrets":
The Mother-Daughter Relationship in
Women's Short Stories

"I think I am in love with my beautiful mother. . . . Sometimes in the streets we have been taken by strangers for sisters. This pleases me much."
—Lucy Howard, 1850s

IN THE JUNE 1888 *LADIES HOME JOURNAL*, THAT STEADY FOUNTAIN OF popular wisdom, Fanny Fern, advised America's young women, "Have no secrets that you would not be willing to trust to your mother. She is your best friend, and is ever devoted to your honor and interest."[1] Any study of nineteenth-century middle-class women's relationship stories must begin with the relationship nineteenth-century mothers and daughters shared, since the mother-daughter bond was the most fundamental, "primitive" relationship in nineteenth-century middle-class women's lives, culture, and communication. In analyzing the private correspondence of middle-class American women, Carroll Smith-Rosenberg notes the centrality of the mother-daughter bond to the nineteenth-century "women's sphere":

> At the heart of this world lay intense devotion and identification between mothers and daughters. Mothers and daughters took joy and comfort in one anothers' presence. They often slept with one another throughout the daughter's adolescence, wept unashamedly at separation, and rejoiced at reunions. Mother-daughter bonding served as the model of subsequent relations with other women.[2]

Indeed, a brief survey of articles appearing in the *Ladies Home Journal* in the late nineteenth century ("True Relationship of Mother and Daughter," "Tell Your Mother," "A Girl's Best Friend," "A Daughter at Home: Helping Her Mother Socially") reveals that not just the dynamics of the mother-daughter tie but the relative "health" of the relationship itself were subjects of vast concern to a popular female audience.[3]

Yet, despite the pervasive interest in mother-daughter issues among women readers, nineteenth-century mother-daughter stories have received surprisingly little critical recognition beyond their recent "rediscovery" by feminist scholars. The apparent oversight is most puzzling in light of the significant research that has been done on Victorian America's obsession with what Mary P. Ryan has called "the empire of the mother." Scholars such as Linda Rosenzweig, Jan Lewis, and Ann Dally have observed that throughout most of the nineteenth century, motherhood was constructed as not just a feminine "ideal," but as the only truly viable role for middle-class American women.[4] Further, Smith-Rosenberg explains that the mother-daughter bond was largely grounded in an "apprenticeship system" through which American mothers passed on to their daughters the gender norms and identities that maintained and perpetuated the mother-ideal.[5] As Nancy M. Theriot explains, "The mother/daughter relationship was the core experience of nineteenth-century feminine acculturation."[6] Given the recent scholarly interest in nineteenth-century motherhood and the cultural significance of the mother-daughter tie, surely women's short fiction presenting this "core experience" would inspire a wave of critical inquiries into the relationship's forms and functions in women's stories?

As Jan Lewis convincingly details, however, the nineteenth-century valorization of motherhood primarily served to meet the needs of middle-class patriarchal order. Asserting that maternal love "was the very basis of the social order, its blood and sinew both,"[7] Lewis explains how the theological and democratic dialectic that shaped nineteenth-century middle-class culture also fashioned the accepted definition of motherhood; "the paradigmatic mother was this dialectic's creature, designed to serve its ends."[8] Within the framework of patriarchal order, then, the "secrets" shared between mothers and daughters—the ways that the relationship itself "works"—are irrelevant to the point of near invisibility. Citing the social forces within the "apprenticeship system" which effectively "marginalize" the mother-daughter bond, Signe Hammer states,

> Because society expects a mother to raise a daughter to be a wife and
> mother in her turn, most of what passes between a mother and daughter

falls outside the acknowledged social context of men-women relationships. This has had the paradoxical effect of making the mother-
daughter relationship an "underground" one, whose emotional power
and importance may be increased precisely because it is "underground,"
with no wider context than the immediately personal through which it
can be channeled into a more conscious and concrete form. What is
taken for granted, and therefore ignored, may be the most powerful.[9]

Hammer's insights reveal the critical perspective necessary to
share the "secrets" within nineteenth-century mother-daughter relationships and short stories. Feminist literary scholars such as Susan
Koppelman have begun exploring the "underground" genre of
women's mother-daughter stories, reclaiming such works from the
realms of "regional" and "sentimental" fiction.[10] Such work, of
course, has been crucial to understanding the true place of mother-
daughter stories in both the women's and the American short story
traditions. But, in considering the appeal of mother-daughter stories
for a *nineteenth-century* popular female audience, we must begin to
question just how this "immediately personal" relationship was "channeled into a more conscious and concrete form" in women's short
fiction. Precisely *what* was "taken for granted" by nineteenth-century
women writers and readers concerning mother-daughter intimacy,
and in what ways did such tacitly understood "secrets" shape women's
storytelling?

Mary E. Wilkins Freeman's "On the Walpole Road" (1884) is an
example of a nineteenth-century mother-daughter story that, at first
glance, may seem to be no "story" at all.[11] Indeed, Freeman deliberately undercuts any sense of linear progression to create a circular
tale that turns in on itself and—at least at a plot level—seems somehow "pointless." "On the Walpole Road" opens with an emphasis on
the familiar, repetitive nature of Mrs. Green and Almiry's trip to and
from the town of Walpole. Despite Almiry's urging with the reins, the
horse refuses to break out if its accustomed trot, and the reader can
almost hear the plodding clop of hooves keeping time with the
rhythms of Mrs. Green's storytelling. Mrs. Green is reminded of her
tale by the weather ("That cloud makes me think of Aunt Rebecca's
funeral"), and the woman ostensibly tells the "story" of "On the Walpole Road" to pass the time: "It'll keep us from getting aggervated at
the horse, poor, dumb thing!" (308)

A familiar device in regionalist fiction, the frame tale often presents "local color" characters such as Mrs. Green as mechanisms through which the "real" story gets told. However, this familiar pattern is strangely disrupted by the apparent pointlessness of Mrs. Green's tale at each level, for the reader is repeatedly led down conventional plot paths only to hit what seems a dead end. The reader is initially led to believe that the frame character will unfold the tale of "Aunt Rebecca's funeral." But she soon learns that this is not the case; Aunt Rebecca's funeral does not take place at all and, in fact, the woman herself is alive throughout most of the interpolated story. Next, the reader might assume that the heart of Mrs. Green's tale is in the ironic (perhaps comic) "mistake" which had led the woman to think that her aunt was dead when actually Uncle Enos had passed away. Yet this plot path too seems to leave the reader nowhere. Upon arriving for her aunt's funeral and seeing the woman alive, Mrs. Green erupts with uncontrollable laughter. She tells Almiry, "But I s'-pose the sudden change from feelin' so bad made me kinder highst-ericky" (310), but beyond this brief explanation and an equally brief description of the mourners' stunned expressions, the scene of Mrs. Green's dramatic "discovery" and the entire "mistaken death" plot pattern fizzle out with no comment.

At this point in the framed tale—with both Mrs. Green and the reader puzzled—Aunt Rebecca calls Mrs. Green aside: "Come into the bedroom with me a minute, Sarah" (310). With the invitation, the reader is also invited to expect an explanatory, "confessional" scene in which long-hidden secrets are shared and the plot is finally made coherent. Yet this traditional plot structure, too, is rejected; Aunt Rebecca makes no startling revelation to Mrs. Green about her loveless marriage to Uncle Enos since, in fact, Mrs. Green had heard the story years earlier. Mrs. Green tells Almiry she "couldn't help wonderin'" (313) if Aunt Rebecca would marry her true love, but she does not ask her aunt, and the woman herself reveals nothing. Mrs. Green comments that her aunt did not appear to have been crying, "But then that wa'n't nothin' to go by" (313), underscoring the fact that Mrs. Green actually learns nothing new in the bedroom scene. What might have served as a typical romantic close to Mrs. Green's tale is subverted by the distinctly anti-romantic (and anticlimactic) ending of Aunt Rebecca's story: Aunt Rebecca does finally marry her true love, but "they wa'n't so happy after all" (313), and Aunt Rebecca soon after dies horribly of cholera-morbus.

Having plodded through the tale of "Aunt Rebecca's funeral," the reader discovers that not only Aunt Rebecca's story but also the frame narrative involving Mrs. Green and Almiry has "gone nowhere." After listening silently to the entire tale, Almiry reveals that Mrs. Green has told this story before, and an undisturbed Mrs. Green replies, "Wa'al, I declare, I shouldn't wonder ef I did" (314). The horse returns "willingly" home (314), the storm that the dark clouds forebode never breaks, and "On the Walpole Road" abruptly comes to a halt having just traveled nowhere and back.

For readers trained in the tradition of Poe's "unity of effect," the apparent lack of cohesion between the parts of Freeman's story can be unsettling. Moreover, the meandering plot of "On the Walpole Road" seemingly violates Poe's principle that a story have an "indispensable air of consequence" with a steady progression toward a certain denouement throughout.[12] Why, then, might a nineteenth-century audience have even *read* such a tale? How does Freeman satisfy her readers' need for the "story" in a short story, even as she deliberately undercuts any overt sense of plot, purpose, or closure? Surely, the story's appeal to a nineteenth-century female readership could not rest exclusively in the local color characters and dialogue, for such an explanation suggests that the content of regionalist fiction was largely discounted. What "story" did nineteenth-century women readers detect in Freeman's now "storyless" tale?

The pattern to follow with "On the Walpole Road" involves recognizing the mother-daughter relationships that permeate the story and are woven so intricately into its fabric that they seem invisible. Susan Koppelman asserts that women writing about mothers and daughters for a female audience "are inferential and notational," since the pattern of communication and interaction "is so familiar to women readers, the writer has great latitude for using the most subtle forms of artistic literary innuendo and ellipses."[13] The "story" in "On the Walpole Road" lies in the subtle interplay of mother-daughter relationships and the murmured tones of mother-daughter communication that resonated for Freeman's readers.

The core mother-daughter relationship in Freeman's story is that between Aunt Rebecca and her mother, since the conflict in this relationship over Rebecca's marriage is the catalyst for the interpolated tale's dramatic action. Although Rebecca loves Abner Lyons, her mother "fairly hated him" and, it is said, "would rather hev buried Rebecca than seen her married to him" (311). Rebecca's mother is set on her daughter having Enos Fairweather and "took on, an' acted so" that Rebecca "jest give in to her," notwithstanding some wedding-day dramatics at the altar. Mary R. Reichardt notes how a struggle between mother and daughter over the daughter's marriage choice is a frequent subject of Freeman's stories, as it is throughout women's fiction.[14] Yet, what is interesting and significant in "On the Walpole Road" is how this crucial mother-daughter conflict is presented so matter-of-factly by Mrs. Green, with surprisingly little elaboration or explanation regarding either the mother's pressure or the daughter's submission. Mrs. Green relates how Rebecca's mother "was dreadful nervous an' feeble" (311), but the actual "story" of how the mother is able to sway Rebecca is never told.

Of course, this "story" would have been well known by nineteenth-century women. While the mother's motives are not directly expressed, her deep-seated need to see Rebecca married to the "right" man surely causes her to "take on so," despite what might seem the obvious contradiction of her daughter's objections. Similarly, Rebecca's desire to please her mother through self-sacrificing obedience echoes loudly the sentiments of many nineteenth-century popular advice articles urging daughters to honor and obey their mothers, even into the daughter's adulthood. For example, in "The Sweetest Word in the Language" (1890), the *Ladies Home Journal* directs American daughters to always address their mothers as "Momma," since a daughter is obliged to give her mother "that pleasure which it should be your duty, every day you live, to give her."[15] The social codes of mother-daughter interaction convey the unstated "story" of Rebecca's marriage; readers attuned to the expectations of this relationship would certainly comprehend what "happens" between Rebecca and her mother and would recognize both women's need to resolve their conflict. In *Between Mothers and Daughters,* Susan Koppelman discusses women's stories in which daughters reject their mothers' marriage choices and thus experience "isolation from the private language and priorities of women's culture."[16] Thus, Freeman's reader might not agree with Rebecca's submission to her mother, but she would certainly understand it.

The bond between mother and daughter also serves to convey the "unsaid" mother-daughter story of Aunt Rebecca and Mrs. Green. In trying to relate to Almiry just how much Aunt Rebecca meant to her, Mrs. Green recalls the woman's great kindness:

"Wa'al you see, Almiry, Aunt Rebecca was my aunt on my mother's side—
my mother's oldest sister she was—an' I'd allers thought a sight of her. . . .
I'll never forget how she nussed me through the typhus fever, the year
after mother died. Thar I was took sick all of a sudden, an' four leetle children cryin', an' Israel couldn't get anybody but that shiftless Lyons
woman, far and near, to come an' help. When Aunt Rebecca heerd of it
she jist left everything an' come. She packed off the Lyons woman, bag
an' baggage, an' tuk right hold, as nobody but her could ha' known how
to. I allers knew I should ha' died ef it hadn't been for her. (308)

Mrs. Green tells Almiry how any prolonged separation from Rebecca
would make her "jist as lonesome an' homesick as could be," and says
that, upon hearing the (incorrect) news of Rebecca's death, "I could-
n't ha' felt much worse ef it had been my mother" (308). With Mrs.
Green's own mother gone, Aunt Rebecca becomes a surrogate
mother to the younger woman, a relationship reinforced by the fact
the Aunt Rebecca never has any children of her own. Koppelman
comments on the recurrence of surrogate-mother figures in women's
fiction, and states that readers' ability to "recognize the [women's]
behavior as mothering" points to a broadly accepted mother-con-
vention at work in both a culture and its fiction.[17]

The mother-daughter bond between the two women makes sense
of Mrs. Green's "highstericky" reaction to the living Rebecca at "Aunt
Rebecca's funeral." At the same time, it lends important insights into
why Mrs. Green is reciting her odd tale to Almiry at all. Mrs. Green
does not bother to explain for Almiry the extreme emotional anguish
and release she experienced at her aunt's "funeral," or the strong
feelings she still has for this "mother." Instead, Mrs. Green relies (to
use Koppelman's phrase) on "what we share as women" to fill in the
vital missing details of this story of Mrs. Green and Aunt Rebecca.[18]
In essence, Mrs. Green assumes that her mother-daughter story will
be a story to Almiry.

The mother-daughter relationship is central to Freeman's frame
device as well. Mrs. Green is made significantly older than Almiry, for
she "might have been seventy" while her listener "was younger—forty
perhaps" (306). Aside from this telling age difference, a mother-
daughter bond is established between Mrs. Green and Almiry
through the act of storytelling itself. Mrs. Green knows the tale of
Aunt Rebecca's loveless match and wedding-day dramatics because "I
heerd about it all from mother" (311). Consequently, Aunt Rebecca's
wedding story takes on an almost legendary quality, as Mrs. Green re-

peats how "Mother said" that Aunt Rebecca looked at the parson "an' her eyes was shinin' an' her cheeks white as lilies," and how "Mother said it was awful," and how "Mother said ef thar was ever anybody looked fit to be a martyr, Aunt Rebecca did then" (312). Signe Hammer notes how knowledge handed down from mother to daughter serves to forge bonds across generations:

> A mother does not merely pass on the messages of her culture; she also passes on her responses to the messages she received from her mother. Thus, every transaction between mother and daughter is in a sense a transaction among three generations.[19]

By further passing along the story of "Aunt Rebecca's funeral" to another generation of women, Mrs. Green presents a story that is, in a sense, self-reflexive; her tale creates mother-daughter ties through its rendering of mother-daughter relationships. The "circular" feel of "On the Walpole Road" is not simply because nothing "happens," but because what does occur in the story is repetitive, cyclical, continuous. Mrs. Green is not disturbed by the revelation that she has told her tale before, since, no doubt, she will tell it again; more than an ironic closing twist, the repetitive aspect of Mrs. Green storytelling is central to the overall structure of "On the Walpole Road." Hammer states, "Mothers of daughters are daughters of mothers and have remained so, in circles joined to circles, since time began."[20] "On the Walpole Road" uses such mother-daughter "circles" to construct the story for a female audience, who now function as the next generation to know the story of "Aunt Rebecca's funeral."

The theme of storytelling's potential to link women's lives across generations is central to Native American writer Zitkala Sa's "The Trial Path" (1901), but in this mother-daughter story the focus is more on what is lost between generations than what is shared.[21] As the story opens, a Native American girl muses aloud to her grandmother that the star peeping into their teepee smoke-hole is the spirit of her dead grandfather. With this, the grandmother is mystically carried back to her youth ("Listen! I am young again . . ."), and she recites as in a trance the tale of her own great crisis. The grandmother tells how her lover murdered his best friend in a dispute over her, and how the guilty man's fate came to depend on successfully riding a wild pony along the trial path. Her eyes closed tight, the old woman relives her ordeal as she paints the living images for her granddaughter:

Ah! I see strong men trying to lead the lassoed pony, pitching and rearing, with white foam flying from his mouth. I choke with pain as I recognize my handsome lover desolately alone, striding with set face toward the lassoed pony. "Do not fall! Choose life and me!" I cry in my breast, but over my lips I hold my thick blanket. (561)

In telling her story, the grandmother confides that the tale contains "the sacred knowledge in [her] heart" which the granddaughter is surely "old enough to understand" (562). The old woman, however, is dismayed to discover that her heart-rending tale has merely put the younger woman to sleep: "Asleep! I have been talking in the dark, unheard. I did wish the girl would plant in her heart this sacred tale" (562–63).

The grandmother relives her torturous experience in an attempt to share her "sacred knowledge," but her granddaughter neither empathizes with the older woman's suffering nor understands the purpose of her grandmother's storytelling. As in "On the Walpole Road," the closing "failure" of the interpolated story is an integral part of not just the frame story but the grandmother's "sacred" tale as well, since the old woman's story gains both power and urgency through the suggestion that it might someday be lost. The inability of the grandmother's story to communicate to the granddaughter itself becomes the story, one grounded in the rapidly changing world of nineteenth-century Native Americans as much as in the world of mother-daughter intimacy. Recognizing and sharing the grandmother's terrible sadness over what is lost between Native American mothers and daughters renders the grandmother's "pointless" tale meaningful to a largely white audience to whom most other elements of the story would be foreign. Zitkala Sa's story operates on the assumption that readers will acknowledge the impact on women's lives of a break in the "circles joined to circles" across generations of women.

Issues of motherly and daughterly "duty" which arise in a story such as "On the Walpole Road" prove key structural devices in many stories by nineteenth-century women. An important aspect of the nineteenth-century mother-ideal was the personal sacrifice involved in mothering, a complete giving of oneself which presumably all "true" women accepted willingly as part of their female destiny. Nancy Theriot notes that the nineteenth-century perception of maternal love's *selflessness* served to elevate the mother-child bond above other relations[22] and to establish maternal sacrifice as a criterion for womanhood itself:

In advice literature, diaries, and popular fiction, women celebrated self-
sacrificing to the point of suffering as part of true womanhood because
this trait was seen as a necessary part of motherhood.[23]

The equation of good womanhood with good motherhood and
the implicit self-abnegation in both interconnected roles were further complicated for middle-class women by the unique psychosocial
configuration of the middle-class mother-daughter bond. Exploring
twentieth-century female interaction, Nancy Chodorow, in *The Reproduction of Motherhood*, contends that because women chiefly occupy
the social position of "mother" in Western culture, the mother-child
relationship is inescapably colored by gender. For a girl, gender identity is formed through a recognition of her sameness to the
mother/love object, a recognition which itself helps ensure that she
will assume a similar social role. A girl's personal identity is bound up
with the mother, resulting in a "merging" of selfhood that Chodorow
claims is experienced equally by the mother; a woman sees her
daughter as an "extension" or "double" of herself.[24]

Chodorow's psychoanalytical approach to mother-daughter intimacy has largely come under attack by scholars who cite the cultural
assumptions informing both Chodorow's research and her theories.
But Chodorow's descriptions of the mother-daughter dyad do prove
useful in analyzing the nineteenth-century American middle-class
"version" of the mother-daughter bond because, as several critics
have observed, Chodorow's theoretical framework mirrors strikingly
middle-class family structure in Victorian America. Theriot writes,

> Among the middle-class, an increasingly private family form developed in
> the nineteenth century, in which the husband left home to work, chil-
> drearing became a focused and private female activity, and women were
> economically dependent. If Chodorow's theory is culture-bound in posit-
> ing a particular family structure as universal, that structure was indeed the
> predominant family type among middle-class nineteenth-century Ameri-
> cans.[25]

Thus, in considering the "selflessness" of middle-class maternal love,
it is important to explore how such sacrifice, when performed for a
daughter, paradoxically translated into a personal gain for the mother
"double." The idealized "fusion" of mother and daughter in the nineteenth-century social code also worked in women's fiction to make

"believable" the extent to which mother figures would act on a daughter's behalf.

The mother-daughter mechanism thus creates in nineteenth-century women's fiction the context in which otherwise inconceivable feats are explicable, accepted, almost expected. The presumption of maternal self-sacrifice informs Edith Wharton's surrogate-mother story, "The Quicksand" (1904), in which a mother sacrifices her son's happiness—and her own carefully constructed complacency—to save a younger "daughter" figure.[26] Despite the son's pleas for help in winning over Hope Fenno, Mrs. Quentin ultimately turns against her son and begs Hope not to marry him. How does Wharton's mother betray her son and purposely thwart his wedding plans while retaining her "motherly" status with a female popular audience?

From the story's outset, Wharton takes great care to stress the "excessive intimacy" (398) shared by Mrs. Quentin and Alan, making the final betrayal of trust seem unlikely. As would be expected, Mrs. Quentin practically lives for her only child, and she responds with "instinctive anger" (398) upon hearing that Hope has refused his proposal. Mrs. Quentin faithfully fulfills her motherly obligation to meet with the girl, and she dutifully takes her son's part in advising Hope to blind herself to Alan's unscrupulous business affairs. But, in the end, this mother takes back her words, professing her "motherly" advice a deliberate lie. In the story's climactic "confessional" scene between Hope and Mrs. Quentin, the older woman reveals her own long-repressed shame and hypocrisy for abandoning her principles in exchange for financial security, and she warns the girl not to follow in her footsteps:

> Do you suppose I'd do this if you were the kind of pink and white idiot he ought to have married? It's because I see you're alive, as I was, tingling with beliefs, ambitions, energies, as I was—that I can't see you walled up alive, as I was, without stretching out a hand to save you! (407)

Mrs. Quentin "untells" her lie to Hope Fenno explicitly because the younger woman so strikingly resembles *Mrs. Quentin* just at the moment of her own fateful mistake. In breaking her long silence and voicing her hypocrisy, Mrs. Quentin must also confront the self-delusions that have made her life bearable, and she tells Hope, "Your face has waked [an aching nerve of truth] in me" (410). The story's "betrayal" is , ironically, a story of maternal sacrifice in which a mother betrays herself in order to rescue her younger "double." Despite the certain guilt from her son's disappointment, Mrs. Quentin sees in Hope a chance to atone for her own duplicity, an opportunity unavailable in even her close relationship with Alan (who, of course, followed in his father's footsteps).

By constructing a surrogate-mother-daughter relationship, then, Wharton redeems this "deceitful" mother, recasting her into a "true" mother/woman and making acceptable the otherwise improbable plot reversal. In "untelling" her lifelong lie, Mrs. Quentin performs exactly the type of personal sacrifice that Wharton's audience would expect from her. In this sense, the surrogate-mother-daughter scenario Wharton paints in "The Quicksand" is similar to a surrogate-father-son relationship in Sherwood Anderson's "The Untold Lie" (1919) in which a young man asks his "old daddy" friend whether or not to marry.[27] In Anderson's story, however, the surrogate-father figure is not willing to "untell" the lie shrouding his ruined life. Instead of sharing a painful self-recognition, he reaffirms the lie to both his "son" and himself. Many women's mother-daughter stories involve the sort of personal sacrifice of a mother figure for a daughter that Anderson's father is incapable of making. For Example, in Fannie Hurst's "Oats for the Woman" (1917), a stepmother reveals a premarital affair (and is consequently cast out by her husband) in order to spare her stepdaughter from marrying the former lover.[28] Surely the nineteenth-century idealization of maternal sacrifice made such fantastic plot twists relatively "realistic" for the stories' audience.

Although nineteenth-century middle-class ideology broadly fused motherhood and womanhood, some scholars have seen the "empire of the mother" as a potential source of power and autonomy for woman. Discussing the attitudes of the Female Moral Reform Society, Smith-Rosenberg notes that most members willingly limited woman to her "sphere" of domestic and spiritual concerns, but also believed strongly that "in these areas her power should be paramount."[29] Similarly, Theriot contends that the mother-centered "script" of true womanhood which defined woman through domesticity also allotted her "a uniquely female avenue of power" in middle-class society.[30] A mother's "power" to protect and provide for her daughter is central to two of Mary E. Wilkins Freeman's most anthologized stories, "The Revolt of 'Mother'" (1891) and "Old Woman

Magoun" (1909). Predictably, the appeal of these stories to contemporary scholars and readers has been the expression of nineteenth-century women's power—or powerlessness—in the face of male oppression. Very likely, however, the stories read by Freeman's intended audience were complicated by mother-daughter issues not readily perceived today.

In "The Revolt of 'Mother'," Sarah Penn somehow musters the courage to move her family into her husband's new barn when the man refuses to build the family a decent house.[31] What has most commonly earned critical interest in this story is how "Mother" *can* revolt; what force drives the quiet, New England housewife to mutiny after forty years of waiting patiently for the long-promised house? Mary Reichardt notes how carefully Freeman details Mrs. Penn's movements to invite us—"the woman reader especially—to read 'between the lines' and participate in mother's moral dilemma."[32] But the question seldom asked of Freeman's tale is how Mother's act functions in the story's overall structure: How does Mother's revolt "work" in the story?

"The Revolt of 'Mother'" opens with a focus on the tension between "Mother's" and "Father's" priorities. When Mrs. Penn demands repeatedly why men are digging near their home, Mr. Penn simply tells her, "I wish you'd go into the house, mother, an' 'tend to your own affairs" (148). Mrs. Penn does "'tend to her affairs," even after learning that a new barn is being erected on the lot where a house was supposed to have been built. Despite her obvious anger, Mother continues her daily tasks of washing dishes, cutting shirts, and baking pies, for "however deep a resentment she might be forced to hold against her husband, she would never fail in sedulous attention to his wants" (151). Sarah Penn is, above all, a *dutiful* woman, even to the extent of defending her husband when their daughter, Nanny, complains about their dilapidated home.

Yet, a vital aspect of Sarah Penn's "affairs" as "Mother" is her duty to her children, and here lies her moral dilemma and the story's dramatic tension. Mrs. Penn calls Father inside and—for the first time in forty years—"talks plain" (152) to her husband, trying to make him comprehend the need for a new house. She points to her bare kitchen and laments that the cramped, carpetless room is all Nanny has for entertaining in, "an' there ain't one of her mates by what's got better" (152). She throws open the door leading to a narrow staircase and says,

> There, father . . . I want you to look at the stairs that go up to them two
> unfinished chambers that are all the places our son an' daughter have had
> to sleep in all their lives. There ain't a prettier girl in town nor a more la-
> dylike one than Nanny, an' that's the place she has to sleep in. (152)

Most importantly, Mrs. Penn wants a new house because Nanny
is soon to be married. She asks her husband to consider what the
girl's wedding will be like in their ramshackle home and tries to make
him understand the true seriousness of the situation:

> An' there's another thing—I ain't complained; I've got along forty years,
> an' I s'pose I should forty more, if it wa' n't for that—if we don't have an-
> other house. Nanny can't live with us after she's married. She'll have to
> go somewheres else to live away from us, an' it don't seem as if I could
> have it so noways, father. . . . She'll be all worn out inside of a year. Think
> of her doin' all the washin' an' ironin' an' bakin' with them soft white
> hands an' arms, an' sweepin'! I can't have it so, noways, father. (152–53)

Concern for her daughter provides Sarah Penn with both the reason
and the courage to break her forty-year silence. Mrs. Penn has always
carried the weight of the domestic cares, and she knows that Nanny
is ill prepared to move away and take on such duties. Mrs. Penn's apparent pampering of her daughter reflects fairly common middle-
class attitudes concerning women's roles as both nurturers and models for their daughters. Theriot writes,

> By facilitating a carefree adolescent lifestyle for daughters, mothers pro-
> vided a lesson in motherly sacrifice for family and reiterated the expecta-
> tions that adult womanhood would soon enough bring such sacrifices to
> daughters. . . . This relatively frivolous adolescence can be seen as a
> mother's final gift to her daughter.[33]

Significantly, however, Mrs. Penn is unwilling to force Nanny into
"womanhood," for she refuses to push her daughter outside the
realm of maternal care into the world of female drudgery. Here, perhaps, lies the most "radical" element of Mrs. Penn's "revolt." While
social norms dictate that Mrs. Penn mold Nanny into a productive,
all-giving mother/woman, Mrs. Penn "rebels," knowingly perpetuat-
ing Nanny's "frivolous adolescence" through her own protracted sacrifice.

"The Revolt of 'Mother'" was terrifically received, earning for
Freeman both popular and critical acclaim. Although modern schol-

ars have emphasized almost exclusiveley its themes of power and sub-version, most have failed to consider fully the story's appeal to the nineteenth-century reader, especially in terms of mother-daughter is-sues. Although Mrs. Penn has never complained openly about their lot, Nanny is comfortable confessing to her mother her embarrass-ment about holding a wedding in the old house, again underscoring the closeness most nineteenth-century women readers would expect between mother and daughter. In a pivotal mother-daughter scene, *Nanny* voices Mrs. Penn's well-checked frustration, peevishly remark-ing, "We might have the wedding in the new barn" (153). Nanny is thus the catalyst for Mother's revolt in a dual sense, since she not only fuels Mrs. Penn's desire for a new house, but unwittingly lights the fire. Although Mrs. Penn's response is immediately obscure to her daughter, the reader is made to understand clearly what Mrs. Penn will ultimately do: "Mrs. Penn had started, and was staring at her with a curious expression. She turned again to her work, and spread out a pattern carefully on the cloth" (153).

The story's "pattern" now spread before the reader, two key ques-tions must be asked. First, how will Freeman make the act that will surely follow "work" for her reader? And second, why would the reader continue on, once the overt plot has been so plainly unveiled? The answer to both questions, once more, rests in the "unsaid" mother-daughter story in "Revolt."

Commenting on "The Revolt of 'Mother'" for the 1917 *Saturday Evening Post,* Freeman claimed that the story hinges on "a big fib"[34] and that "essential truth" had been compromised in the tale:

> There never was in New England a woman like Mother. If there had been she most certainly would not have moved into the palatial barn which her husband had erected next to the mean little cottage she had occupied during her married life. She simply would have lacked the nerve. She would also have lacked the imagination.[35]

Nonetheless, the believability of Mother's act within the reality of the story is never in question, even as the narrator emphasizes the fan-tastic nature of the event. Indeed, Freeman takes great pains to im-press on her reader the "uncanny and superhuman quality" of the feat performed "by this simple, pious New England mother" (156), paralleling her heroism to that of the Pilgrim Fathers. Just moments before Mrs. Penn sets her plan in motion, Freeman once more re-minds the reader of the mother-daughter concerns behind the move:

Nanny sat sewing. Her wedding-day was drawing nearer, and she was getting pale and thin with her steady sewing. Her mother kept glancing at her.
   "Have you got that pain in your side this mornin' ?" she asked.
   "A little."
   Mrs. Penn's face, as she worked, changed, her perplexed forehead
smoothed, her eyes were steady, her lips firmly set . . . she made up her
mind to her course of action. (154–55)

To a female audience schooled in the ideal of motherhood's limitless
selflessness, Mrs. Penn's revolt is not unreasonable. However, Father,
who is outside the mother-daughter realm, has "no idee" (159) how
far Mother will go; he is completely shaken and ultimately shattered
by the magnitude of her intent. Significantly, however, Freeman's audience cannot share in such shock and disbelief. Mother's revolt succeeds as a "story" precisely because of its mother-daughter underpinnings, for, without them, Mrs. Penn's deed would have been
dismissed as unbelievable—or, more likely, condemned as unaccept-
able—by a nineteenth-century female audience.
   The relative morality of Mrs. Penn's actions suggests an answer to
the second question posed concerning the story's continued appeal
even after the plot "twist" is revealed. A woman reader who both understands and shares Mother's sentiments would surely feel that her
motives are worthy and her actions justified. Of course, such a reader
would thus look forward to witnessing Mother's final triumph and
vindication. Still, Freeman skillfully taps into the anxiety a nineteenth-century female audience would experience with Mother's
success, for such a reader would not likely want to see Father (an essentially "good" man) hurt in the process. The real challenge for Mrs.
Penn—and the unsaid "story" for the nineteenth-century reader—
lies in balancing a woman's two most important social roles as wife
and mother. While her priorities will prevail, Mother cannot lose her
status as Mrs. Penn and remain sympathetic and admirable to a nineteenth-century audience. Thus, the "story" for Freeman's reader,
which does not work in the same way today, is how Mrs. Penn will "pull
it off." The dilemma's outcome is fraught with ambiguity both for
Mrs. Penn and Freeman's reader; indeed, with the closing image of
Father and Mother crying, an nineteenth-century woman reader
most likely needed to remind herself that Mrs. Penn was right.
   Scholars such as Mary P. Ryan have challenged the notion of separate spheres as a power base for women, noting how women's rela-

tive isolation and narrow social space rendered their alliances largely ineffectual.[36] While Mrs. Penn "wins" in "The Revolt of 'Mother',," the mother's triumph in "Old Woman Magoun" is much more dubious and the mother-daughter bond made significantly problematic.

Much like the opening lines of "Revolt," "Old Woman Magoun's" overt plot begins with the contrast between men's and women's work: Old Woman Magoun sees the need for a bridge across Barry River, but as a woman she can only chide the men around her into action, claiming she would do the work herself if she "were a *man*."[37] This focus on the boundary between male and female worlds quickly shifts to inside the women's sphere and the relationship between the old woman and her granddaughter, Lily. In keeping with social convention, Old Woman Magoun has modeled Lily after herself, teaching Lily "everything she knew" and impressing on the girl the virtues of obedience, honesty, and industriousness (160). Yet, at the same time the reader is encouraged to recognize Old Woman Magoun's dutiful attention to her granddaughter, she is also compelled to question this mother's "mothering" when faced with the product of her handiwork. Even though Lily is fourteen, Old Woman Magoun insists "she's nothin' but a baby" (161), and she keeps the girl in near infancy, isolating her from other children, allowing her to hold on to her rag doll, dressing her in little-girl clothes. The absurd image of this child/woman coupled with the rumors surrounding Lily's birth (Lily's mother was seduced and abandoned at sixteen) suggest that Old Woman Magoun—for all her genuine love and attention—may have somehow failed in her motherly duty to her daughters. In a culture that glorified motherhood's formative influence, especially on girls, the degree to which Old Woman Magoun successfully apprenticed her daughters would be a pivotal "story" in the tale. While Mrs. Penn protects Nanny from the hard domestic toil of a woman's "career," Old Woman Magoun refuses to prepare her daughters for the sexual demands of the role, "babying" Lily (and perhaps Lily's mother as well) in an effort to deny completely the girl's approaching entrance into the world of men.

Indeed, Lily unwittingly strays into trouble and sets the mechanism for her own trap precisely *because* of her grandmother's failure to teach her about men and sexuality. When the old woman sends Lily on her fateful trip to the store, she once more instructs the girl to talk to no one, but "of course, if anybody speaks to you answer them polite, and then come right along" (161). Such advice proves useless in Lily's encounter on the road with the "nice man" (162) whose friendly conversation not only has ulterior motives but stirs Lily's own awakening sexuality. Still, as in "The Revolt of 'Mother',", women's relative power and their ability to protect their daughters is ambiguous. When Lily's father decides to "collect" the girl in order to pay off a gambling debt to another man, it is clear to both Old Woman Magoun and the reader that no "apprenticeship system" could painlessly acculturate Lily into the humiliating world of sexual exploitation that awaits her.

Unwilling to see another daughter lost to male depravity, Old Woman Magoun exercises her only "power" and silently looks away as Lily eats poisonous berries. As in "Revolt," Freeman foreshadows her plot's outcome relatively early. On their walk to Lawyer Mason's, the grandmother and granddaughter pass a stone wall overgrown with "a lusty spread of deadly nightshade full of berries":

> "Those berries look good to eat, grandma," Lily said.
> At that instant the old woman's face became something terrible to see. "You can't have any *now*," she said, and hurried Lily along [emphasis added]. (167)

As in "The Revolt of 'Mother',", two important questions arise with the premature disclosure of the story's ending. Of course, the reader wonders if the old woman will follow through with her apparent plan and reads on to confirm the suspicions raised by the introduction of the nightshade berries. But, more importantly, the reader at this point questions how the old woman *can* poison Lily and remain a sympathetic character. And here, "Old Woman Magoun's" mother-daughter story proves central; for, if Old Woman Magoun loses the reader's sympathy, even momentarily, she is monstrous and the story becomes a tale of abnormal psychology, criminal deviance, "evil stepmother" horror. Freeman makes her story of Lily's sacrifice "work" through the mother-daughter themes that silently pervade the tale.

To begin, Freeman places between the introduction of the nightshade berries and Lily's inevitable taking of them the scene at Lawyer Mason's house. In a desperate attempt to save Lily from sexual exploitation, Old Woman Magoun tries to persuade the lawyer and his wife to adopt the girl. Despite the appeals of both the old woman and Mrs. Mason (who years earlier lost her own little girl), Lawyer Mason will not even consider taking in the illegitimate child. Freeman's quick scene works to impress on the reader the fact that the old woman has no *alternatives* in deciding Lily's fate—not just that no one else will take Lily, but that in this male-dominated world a mother's priorities carry no weight. For all her bluster and belligerence, Old Woman Magoun actually is powerless outside her "women's sphere," and her undaunted determination to fend off threats to her daughter both explains and "justifies" the extremity of her actions. The mother-daughter story in "Old Woman Magoun" demonstrates that the middle-class mother-ideal was a construct used, when convenient, to uphold patriarchal order. In Freeman's story, however, the mother redefines the "sacrifice" tenet of true motherhood/womanhood to meet *women's* priorities and needs.

Indeed, the mother-daughter stories embedded in "Old Woman Magoun" subvert the very climax of the overt plot, the "sacrifice" of Lily. The child's slow, painful death is recast by the grandmother as a return to her mother:

> You will come to a gate with all the colors of the rainbow . . . and it will open, and you will go right in and walk up the gold street, and cross the field where the blue flowers come up to your knees, until you find your mother, and she will take you home where you are going to live. (170)

If Old Woman Magoun is exonerated of Lily's death, it is largely through this continuity of mother-daughter bonds; the child is merely passing from the love and protection of one mother to another, a "changing of hands" that is tellingly contrasted to the proposed sale of the girl by her father.

Nonetheless, as in "The Revolt of 'Mother'," the mother-daughter plot also lends itself to the story's closing moral ambiguity. A nineteenth-century woman reader inundated with popular literature about mentoring daughters would doubtless sense from the outset that something dreadful would befall the pathetically childlike Lily. Ironically, Lily's debased father voices such "motherly" concerns, chiding Old Woman Magoun for keeping Lily a baby and suggesting that the girl's very innocence could lead her into trouble. As the grandmother leads Lily along their fateful path, the girl complains, "You hurt me holding my hand so tight, grandma" (169). Freeman's audience would thus read the final image of the ruined old woman carrying the dead girl's rag doll more like a cautionary message than a closing ironic twist.

Just as the nineteenth-century mother-ideal defined appropriate motherly duty, it simultaneously created pressures on middle-class young women to adhere to a complementary "daughter-ideal" and become the "apprentice" to middle-class womanhood that the "empire of the mother" paradigm advocated. For many middle-class daughters, the wholehearted obedience, intimacy, and companionship broadly expected from daughters were spontaneous, pleasurable, largely unproblematic aspects of their mother-daughter relationships. Smith-Rosenberg's investigation into the "female world of love and ritual" cites numerous examples of middle-class daughters seemingly having little difficulty living the daughter-ideal and, in fact, delighting in the physical and emotional closeness that they and their mothers shared. But the very fact that a writer such as Fanny Fern would need to "remind" American daughters of their obligation to confide in Mother reveals that such a daughterly duty was not always accepted willingly. Apparently some nineteenth-century young women experienced the "blurring" of identities in mother-daughter bonding that Chodorow describes as a source of considerable tension, particularly concerning a mother's control over a daughter's life choices. In an early 1890s lecture "A Daughter's Duty," Charlotte Perkins Gilman stated:

> A duty is a duty, but there is more than one way of doing it! A girl can take care of her mother as an independent householder and wage earner, providing her with the same delicate generosity, let us hope with which the mother once "supported" her; or she can take care of her as a subordinate, a nurse, a companion, upper servant. Why is not the first better? . . . The object of this is to suggest to the Daughter that she is also an Individual and a Human Being, and has duties as an individual to herself, and as a human being to her race, as well as the duty of a daughter to her mother.[38]

As several mother-daughter stories illustrate, the concurrent and contradictory pressures of identification and autonomy in the mother-daughter relationship rendered the role of the nineteenth-century daughter an especially complex mechanism for conveying meaning in fiction. Daughterhood could provide identity and belonging; it could also result in entrapment, exploitation, and painful loss of freedom. For the woman reader, then, the "double-edged" power of the daughter-ideal constituted the "unsaid" story in many mother-daughter tales.

The "unsaid" in Susan Pettigru King Bowen's "A Marriage of Persuasion" (1857) speaks directly to the conflicts and ambiguities many women knew as part of mother-daughter intimacy, since Bowen's story focuses on how a mother can "persuade" her daughter to marry a man whom the girl does not love.[39] The story opens after Anna has refused Mr. Gordon's proposal, and the dramatic tension (which will increase steadily throughout the story) is immediately cast as a conflict of wills between mother and daughter:

> "Then, *why* can't you marry Mr. Gordon, and make me happy?"
> "Because," and Anna's voice was firm, decided and honest. "Because I do not love him, and to marry him would make me very unhappy." (16)

Mrs. Mansfield, however, is equally decided that Anna has rejected an excellent husband, and points out to her daughter the financial benefits of the match:

> "Ah, my dear," said Mrs. Mansfield, "you know how poor we are now. Here I am with you four girls, and an income not much larger than in your dear father's time I spent upon my own dress. Is it wonderful that I long to see you settled?" (17)

Koppelman cites "A Marriage of Persuasion" as an example of stories featuring mothers who teach their girl children to "sell themselves" and who seemingly collaborate "in breaking their daughters to the will of the patriarchy."[40] But Koppelman's comments assume that the story here is the "selling off" of Anna Mansfield. Her reading also suggests that both mother and daughter are "wrong," Mrs. Mansfield in her unreasonable demands and Anna in her final compliance. Would a nineteenth-century reader likewise condemn the mother-daughter "apprenticeship system" at work in the story? And would such a reader see Bowen's tale as a commentary on motherhood's oppressive influence or a call for daughters to assert their own desires?

The opening mother-daughter conflict of "A Marriage of Persuasion" presents the reader with a "no-win" situation (no real compromise alternative is available), thus ensuring the story's unhappy ending from the outset. For a woman reader familiar with the mother-daughter dynamic, the "story" then becomes *which* woman's sense of duty will prevail. Indeed, for Bowen's audience, the story's true complexity doubtless rested in the fact that both mother and daughter are "right" in terms of motherly/daughterly duty.

To begin, Mrs. Mansfield truly believes that Mr. Gordon will make a good husband, for reasons that go beyond his financial stability. She tells her daughter,

> Heaven knows that I am not one of those mercenary mothers who would give their children to any man with money. No, indeed. I would not be so wicked. But when a gentleman like Norman Gordon—an honorable, trustworthy, generous creature—wishes to become my son, do you wonder that I should desire it too? I knew his father before him—I knew his mother—all good people; it is good blood, my child—the best dependence in the world. (17)

In addition, Mrs. Mansfield tries to make Anna understand her "horror" of "love matches" and to impress on her "how many a girl goes to her ruin by that foolish idea"; Mrs. Mansfield tells her daughter, "I want to save you from this" (18). Clearly, Mrs. Mansfield is considering more than her daughter's economic well-being in her desire to marry Anna to Mr. Gordon. Significantly, in rejecting the notion of "love matches," Mrs. Mansfield is passing along to her daughter the ideals learned from her own mother: "I tell you what I heard from *my* mother, and what every right-minded person knows. 'Make a good choice in life; marry, and love will come afterward' (18). Mrs. Mansfield considers it her motherly duty so to instruct her daughter, and she likewise sees it as Anna's duty to obey, telling the girl,

> Your mother is here to guide and direct you. No good ever comes of a child arguing and setting herself up in this manner to teach those older and wiser than herself. The Bible says, "Honor thy father and thy mother"—it don't say, "dispute with them." (18)

Initially, Anna is headstrong, and her refusal to acquiesce to Mrs. Mansfield's wishes is perceived by the mother as a failure in daughterly duty. This is important, since the psychological "persuasion" that dominates the rest of the story and results in Anna's final "surrender" is a product of the reciprocity of duty implied in the women's relationship. In "The Marriage of Persuasion," when Mrs. Mansfield realizes that appeals to reason will not avail, the mother "change[s] her tactics" and preys on Anna's unavoidable feelings of guilt in disappointing both her mother and society's expectations of the ideal daughter:

[Mrs. Mansfield] no longer scolded or insisted; her reproaches were silent looks of misery—pathetic appeals to heaven "to grant her patience under her afflictions." She was very affectionate to her daughter—heart-rendingly so. Anna was called upon constantly to notice what a tender parent she was distressing. (19)

Bowen's mother-daughter story sheds light on how the mother in "On the Walpole Road," merely by "taking on so," can "persuade" Aunt Rebecca to marry against her will. In each story, the threatened loss of motherly love and approval is more emotionally painful to the girl than the prospect of a loveless marriage, and ultimately the "wearying, petty, incessant, pin-pricks" (21) of guilt have their desired effect. Devoid of its nineteenth-century mother-daughter context, the behavior of these mothers is hardly justifiable, perhaps bordering on selfish cruelty. A daughter's desire to please such a mother is equally "twisted," and "A Marriage of Persuasion" becomes little more than the one-dimensional story of female oppression many feminist scholars see today. A nineteenth-century woman reader, however, would not separate the story's central conflict from its mother-daughter context; for her, Bowen's story "works" precisely because both mother and daughter are real and recognizable. Indeed, Bowen's omniscient narrator interrupts her tale just prior to Anna's "surrender" to underscore the reader's own affinity to the girl:

Let those who blame Anna Mansfield for her next step, pray to be kept from the same pit-fall. This is a mere sketch; but an outline to which all who choose may fill up the hints given. Those who believe that *they* would have been steadfast to the end, will have my admiration, if, when their day of trial comes, they hold firmly to the right. (21)

The female reader—to whom these comments clearly are directed—relies on her understanding of the mother-daughter relationship to complete the story's "outline" and "fill up the hints given." Without such understanding, the story's plot offers ridiculously simplistic "advice" to mothers and daughters ("Don't sell off your daughter," "Don't allow your mother to sway your thinking") which most women readers would surely find worthless. Instead, the mother-daughter story in "A Marriage of Persuasion" presents the complex, sometimes "darker" side of this idealized nineteenth-century relationship.

The emotional repercussions of disobeying Mother underlie the dramatic action of Elizabeth Stuart Phelps's "Old Mother Goose" (1873), a story in which the "double-edged" quality of the daughter-ideal is, perhaps, more sharply drawn than in Bowen's tale.[41] Koppelman calls "Old Mother Goose" the "grandmother" of the "disgraceful mother" genre, stories that portray unconventional (and typically, immoral) mothers and their daughters' efforts to come to terms with such women.[42] At sixteen, Nell Mathers runs away from her wretched, drunken prostitute mother and "recreates" herself into the glamorous and internationally acclaimed opera diva, "Helene Thamre." The "unsaid" in Phelps's story are the forces that compel Thamre to return to her past and confront her mother despite her apparently successful repudiation of both.

At first glance, Thamre's decision to return to her hometown (which no longer recognizes her) and sing in its Christmas pageant seems inexplicable, and the story's opening lines emphasize the puzzling nature of the decision: "When Thamre consented to sing for the citizens of Havermash last year, nobody was more surprised than the citizens of Havermash themselves" (24). Indeed, Thamre herself wonders, "Heaven knows what restless fancy forced me here" (32). Of course, her need to resolve her feelings for the mother she abandoned "force" Thamre back, as evidenced by the singer's request, even before she sees her mother in person, that her performance fee "go to old women who haven't lived as they'd ought to in this town" (25). When Thamre does finally see her mother, the old woman is a "sorry sight," the object of public contempt and vicious attacks by neighborhood boys:

> Old Mother Goose was sitting stupidly in the slush beside the hack-stands. Her shawl was off, her gray hair was fallen raggedly upon her shoulders; her teeth chattered with chill and rage; there were drops of blood about her on the snow . . . (28)

Although Thamre is horrified by the sight, she feels again "the old, old, hateful shame" (34) and resists the impulse to acknowledge her ties to Old Mother Goose. In returning to her mother while outwardly denying her, Thamre demonstrates the ambivalence which Charlotte Perkins Gilman would later suggest at times characterized young women's feelings about daughterly duty, and her tortured protests against her mother's claims on her match tellingly Gilman's sentiments regarding a daughter's duty to herself: "What have you ever done for me, that you should demand a right so cruel? You have no right, I say; you have no right!" (34).

Despite such emotional wrangling, Thamre's return to Haver-mash makes her confrontation with the old woman almost inevitable, and the dramatic reuniting of mother and daughter is set in religious tones in keeping with the story's broader purpose as a Christmas tale. Old Mother Goose interrupts Thamre's singing of "If God Be For Us" to cry, "If God be for me, my girl won't be against me! My girl can't be against me!" (39). Although Mother Goose is a wretchedly "fallen" woman, her ironic title emphasizes the persistent power of her role as "Mother" and explains Thamre's closing self-sacrifice in publicly recognizing their ties. "Old Mother Goose" demonstrates how a daughter's quest for identity necessarily leads back to mother, and contrasts the female values of continuity and connectedness with the largely male (and presumably "American") tradition of independence and self-reliance. Thamre has attained wealth and fame, but she can never achieve fulfillment and true selfhood until she accepts the doctrine of true womanhood and becomes a dutiful daughter; even her stage name betrays her, "Helene Thamre" a mere rearrangement of the letters in "Nell Mathers" to create "the beautiful, false image" (34).

This tacit connection between nineteenth-century motherhood and womanhood structures Grace Elizabeth King's "One of Us" (1893) as well.[43] The dramatic plot of King's story is typical of many nineteenth-century didactic tales preaching the value of female virtue as manifested in a quiet life of helping others. In fact, the story opens with an apparent indictment of "career" women, as represented in the pathetic figure of an opera singer seeking work at an orphanage:

> Yes, one could see her, in that time-honored thin silk dress of hers stiffened into brocade by buckram underneath; the high, low-necked waist, hiding any evidence of breast, if there were such evidences to hide, and bringing the long neck into such faulty prominence; and the sleeves, crisp puffs of tulle divided by bands of red velvet, through which the poor lean arms run like wire, stringing them together like beads. (391)

The orphanage proprietor who narrates the story stresses repeatedly the *falseness* of the woman before her, noting

> the bright little rouge spots in the hollow of her cheek, the eyebrows well accentuated with paint, the thin lips rose-tinted, and the dull, straight hair

frizzled and curled and twisted. . . . Yes, it was she the whilom *dugazon* of the opera troupe. Not that she ever was a *dugazon,* but that was what her voice once aspired to be: a *dugazon manquee* would better describe her. (390–91)

Above all, the narrator's thoughts linger on the assumed shallowness of the young woman's life on the stage, dubbing such women "ghost[s]," the "mere evaporations of real women" (391). With these opening comments, King invites her reader to expect a fairly conventional "fallen woman" story and positions the opera singer outside the women's sphere and subject to any "real" woman's judgment and scorn.

The narrator's thoughts take an interesting turn, however, and it is in this unexpected reversal that the real story lies. As the singer recites "a short story of her life," the narrator is only half-listening; she is so sure of her familiarity with the singer's story that she allows her own thoughts on the singer's falseness to "distract [her] from listening" (391). Similarly, the reader—encouraged by the narrator's comments to believe that she has heard this cliched tale before—might also "half-listen" to "One of Us'" conventional moralizing. Yet there is something striking in the singer's story that draws the narrator back from her thoughts and subsequently causes her to alter completely her opinion of the singer. Indeed, the narrator later acknowledges that her prejudice nearly kept her "from following what was perhaps more profitable" (391) in the singer's tale. The narrator's judgment changes, as does the story's overall structure, "the instant [the singer] spoke of children as she did" (394).

Interpolated into the expected fallen woman story is a mother-daughter tale that works to subvert the more conventional frame structure. The singer tells the narrator how she has "always resisted" the powerful "temptation" to care for children, and she speaks passionately of caring for them: "I dream of it. . . . Their little arms, their little faces, their little lips!" (393). The opera singer tries urgently to make the narrator understand that her true desires can no longer be denied:

"The longing came over me yesterday: I thought of it on the stage, I thought of it afterward—it was better than sleeping; and this morning"— her eyes moistened, she breathed excitedly—"I was determined." (393)

The singer desires a position at the orphanage because "you have more children here than I ever saw anywhere" (394), but she is also attracted to the motherless expressly because she wants to "mother" them; pleading with the orphanage proprietor, she states that when she would love and care for the children, "They would not know but what their mother was there!" (393). Most important, the opera singer longs to mother *daughters,* telling the narrator, "I would ask nothing but my clothes and food, and very little of that; the recompense would be the children—the little girl children" (393). The sincerity of this desire to mother daughters distinguishes the singer's tale from the countless others the narrator has encountered and keeps the woman from dismissing the singer's story "half-heard." To this extent, the singer's story only *becomes* a story for the narrator when the singer introduces mother-daughter themes.

King's female audience was likely won over in a similar manner. Significantly, before the singer touches on the mother-daughter bond she is, essentially, "not real" to the narrator; she is a "ghost," a "sham attendant on sham sensations," a "piece of stage property" (392). The singer's voicing of mother-daughter sentiments makes her a "real" woman to the narrator and grants her entrance into the orphanage's circle of mother-daughter relationships. The tale's narrator thus models the identification process King surely intended her reader to follow, recognizing and validating the singer's desire to become "one of us" through the listener's shared priorities.

Both King and Phelps utilize readily recognizable "woman saved" plots to outline their respective tales. Indeed, there is no question in either story that the "fallen" woman will be redeemed and transformed into a character with whom the audience can at least sympathize. However, "One of Us" and "Old Mother Goose" appropriate the predictability of the "woman saved" convention and ultimately subvert it to tell instead mother-daughter stories. In Phelps's story, the fallen woman is saved not through refound virtue (there is no real indication that Old Mother Goose has "repented") but through the old woman's restored *motherhood.* Similarly, Thamre saves herself from someday becoming the supposed "dugazon manquee" of King's tale not by forsaking the stage but by reclaiming her identity as "daughter." And, in "One of Us," the world-weary opera singer renounces her former life not merely for Christian charity but explicitly for the role of foster-mothering daughters. The "story" in both texts is the re-creation of selfhood through women's re-entrance into the mother-daughter realm.

Interesting comparisons can be made between the "disgraceful" mothers in such middle-class white women's stories and the "disgraceful" mother figure in "After Many Days: A Christmas Story" (1902) by the African-American writer Fannie Barrier Williams.[44] To begin, both stories are Christmas stories overtly designed to convey holiday cheer and Christian benevolence. Yet important plot differences in these "disgraceful mother" stories point to the ways in which African-American women's experiences shaped both mother-daughter ties and tales. In *Invented Lives: Narratives of Black Women, 1860–1960,* Mary Helen Washington writes:

> If there is a single distinguishing feature of the literature of black women—and this accounts for their lack of recognition—it is this: their literature is about black women; it takes the trouble to record the thoughts, words, feelings, and deeds of black women, experiences that make the realities of being black in America look very different from what men have written.[45]

Of course, just as in the case of white women's stories, the dominant cultural biases concerning literary "worth" are vital considerations in examining the critical devaluation of black women's works; if white women's stories seemed "trivial" to editors and scholars, then surely the tales of black women's lives would receive even less regard. In some respects, however, the unabashed sexism and racism operating to devalue black women's stories have overshadowed structural considerations that contributed to the stories' relative obscurity, issues tied directly to women's use of female relationships to create meaning in their short fiction.

As Peter Bruck has observed, W. E. B. DuBois' idea of "double consciousness" has become the dominant metaphor of the African-American artist whose "bicultural condition" makes unclear the writer's "proper audience."[46] The problem with the prevailing "double consciousness" paradigm is twofold: First, it has tended to obscure critical gender considerations by suggesting that black men and women share similar experiences. Second, exaggerated attention is at times paid to the ways African-American writers appeal or do not appeal to white audiences, neglecting the *black woman's* reading of the story and thus the work's full context. In what ways does a writer such as Fannie Barrier Williams use the mother-daughter relationship to make her story "work" for the white and black readers of *Colored American Magazine?*

Initially, "After Many Days " is very much in keeping with the recognizable nineteenth-century tragic mulatta plot: graceful, wealthy,
and strikingly beautiful, Gladys Winne is stunned to learn that Aunt
Linda, an old "yellow" servant, actually is her own grandmother. Despite Aunt Linda's urging to keep this "taint" hidden, Gladys decides
that she cannot so deceive her fiance Paul, and the remainder of the
story tells of the lovers' resolve to overcome even this great obstacle.
However, unlike the more conventional tragic mulatta plot,
Williams's mixed-raced woman does not end unhappily, in part because of her renewed status as a daughter. Gladys decides that she
must tell Paul about Aunt Linda,

> ". . . and if he does not advise me, yes, command me, to own and cherish
> that lonely old woman's love, and make happy her declining years, then
> he is not the man to whom I can or will entrust my love and life." (48)

In her willingness to sacrifice her relationship with Paul in favor of
one with her grandmother, Gladys demonstrates the strength and
self-determination frequently absent in tragic mulatta heroines. Significantly, Gladys's daughterly duty to Aunt Linda is in direct response to the grandmother's own maternal love and sacrifice, and
here Williams's story subverts the conventional "disgraceful mother"
plot as well. Unlike Phelps's Old Mother Goose, Aunt Linda is "disgraceful" only in the terms of a racist society; in terms of the nineteenth-century mother-ideal, Aunt Linda is a remarkably dutiful
mother. The woman explains that she allowed Gladys's father to
"[tear] you from my breaking heart, case it was best" (45), and she
denies her own lonely longing to ever seek out the girl. Aunt Linda
has kept as sacred relics each piece of Gladys's infant wear, and when
the girl discovers the truth of their ties, Aunt Linda's only thoughts
are for Gladys's well-being: "O my God, why did you let her fin me?"
(45). Williams makes clear the tremendous sacrifice the woman has
endured, both in giving up her granddaughter and in keeping their
relation a well-guarded secret.

Such mother-daughter underpinnings are crucial to the story's
central reversal, for Gladys's closing acceptance of her new identity is
in sharp contrast to her initial denial and repulsion. Looking with dis-
gust at Aunt Linda's rude cabin, Gladys sobs, "And I am part of all this!
O, my God, how can I live" (46). When her grandmother tries to con-
sole her by pointing to her affluent upbringing, Gladys cries "with the

utmost contempt," "Gold, gold, what is gold to such a heritage as this? an ocean of gold cannot wash away this stain" (46). For Williams's female audience, the themes of motherly/daughterly sacrifice no doubt played a role in "rationalizing" the plot's somewhat improbable "happy ending": That Aunt Linda has been such a "good" mother creates the expectation that Gladys will reciprocate her kindness in this mother-daughter story, notwithstanding all that separates them. Barbara Christian, among others, has discussed how the mulatta's overt identity as a white rendered her an appealing, sympathetic character to nineteenth-century white readers, a subtle assurance that this daughter, despite her heritage, is indeed "one of us."[47]

For Williams's black readers, however, the mother-daughter story is complicated by race in a way not immediately available to white readers, most notably through the irony of a mother and daughter who are of "different" races. For black women readers, Gladys's identification with "mother" is bound up with identification with her race, a "story" for black women which most likely did not speak to white women readers in the same ways. While Thamre nurses Old Mother Goose through her dying days, the story closes with the young singer returning to the stage, unscathed by her association with her "fallen" mother. However, in "After Many Days," the mother-daughter bond has much more permanent and far-reaching repercussions; acknowledging her ties to Aunt Linda recasts Gladys in a way no one in the story can wholly control. In the end, Gladys's fiance decides to stick by her, since "when would she need his love, his protection, his tenderest sympathy so much as now?" (50). For black women readers, the "love conquers all" ending—so much a staple in white women's popular fiction—must have rung somewhat false in the face of the realities of racial discrimination. African-American women's experience adds a new wrinkle to the disgraceful mother plot, one that cannot so easily be ironed out through any individual's love—even in a Christmas story.

Like many mother-daughter stories by white women, Adeline F. Ries's "Mammy: A Story" (1917) relies heavily on readers' acceptance of the lengths a mother will go on her daughter's behalf to supply the motive for the dramatic action.[48] In Ries's story, however, the middle-class mother convention itself becomes the "story" for women readers. Although Mammy is deeply saddened when her "white baby" Sheila marries, she is comforted by the continued company of her own "black baby" Lucy (80). Mammy's complacency is destroyed, though, when her Lucy is sold away to Sheila to act as "Mammy" to Sheila's newborn son. When, soon after, Lucy dies of heart failure, the stunned, embittered mother can only repeat over and over to herself, "They took her from me an' she died" (82). Mammy goes to Sheila's home and, while the others are at Lucy's funeral, she carries Sheila's infant from the house and tosses him into the sea. Hours later, Mammy is found wandering the beach shouting madly, "They took her from me an' she died."

Without question, "Mammy" is a chilling story and its sheer brevity (just under 1,000 words) adds to the startling harshness of its effect. Yet, interestingly, Ries's main character is not the monstrous figure most readers might expect of a baby-killer; indeed, the story's closing image of the raving Mammy seems much more pathetic than contemptible, an effect that is largely achieved through the repetition of (and, thus, focus on) Mammy's version of the episode: "They took her from me an' she died." Ries defuses Mammy's otherwise inflammatory act by contextualizing the action within the idealized-mother convention, forcing the reader to recognize Mammy's status as mother *before* presenting her with Mammy's crime.

As Ries's title suggests, the "story" lies in her main character's ironic identity as "Mammy," the non-mother caretaker of white babies in the Southern plantation culture. That Mammy is not a *true* mother (even a surrogate one) in this system is demonstrated in Sheila's purchase of Lucy, a biting betrayal that makes plain the complete lack of reciprocity in Mammy's and Sheila's "mother-daughter" relationship; daughterly duty is owed only to mothers.

Whereas the tale's action is, in any context, disturbing, the pivotal "story" here is the assertion of the old woman's motherhood in bitter defiance of the "Mammy" role. When Lucy dies, Mammy refuses to define the event in any terms other than those of the mother-daughter bond: "They took her from me an' she died." In this context, the pseudo-mother-daughter relationship with Sheila is a stinging mockery. Mammy tosses Sheila's infant into the sea "with a shrill cry of 'Up she goes, Sheila'" (83), casting off her Mammy persona and identifying herself wholly as a wronged, embittered mother. Only through this move—the recasting of "Mammy" as the true mother of her own daughter—can Ries provide an understandable (and, perhaps, "justifiable") motive for her readers. Just moments before she acts, and with the baby in her arms, Mammy states that she cannot go to Lucy's funeral and asks Sheila to go in her place: "And

Sheila thought that she understood the poor woman's feelings and
without even pausing to kiss her child she left the room and joined
the waiting slaves" (83). Ries's point, of course, is that Sheila does *not*
"understand" either Mammy's feelings or her intentions. For Ries's
African-American women readers, exploding the "Mammy" myth
and, subsequently, asserting the validity of black mother-daughter
ties was doubtless an essential "story" in the tale.

In discussing the popular nineteenth-century mother-ideal and
its meanings for middle-class women, Theriot writes,

> The child-centered mother was not only promised power and influence,
> she was also promised complete feminine fulfillment. . . . Popular writers
> described motherhood as woman's most complete happiness, on the one
> hand, and as her only source of adult status, on the other.[49]

In Alice Brown's "The Way of Peace" (1898), a woman uses her psychological affinity to her mother to reject the pathetic "old maid"
status society assigns her and to take on instead a more "adult" role.[50]
After her mother's death, Lucy Ann, left "quite alone" (45) in their
house, wonders aloud how she will ever cope with her terrible loss:
"'Oh, I never can bear it!' she said pathetically, under her breath. 'I
never can bear it in the world!'" (46). Lucy Ann's mechanism
for "bearing it" and living without Mother is, instead, to live "with"
her. Even before her mother dies, Lucy Ann is aware of her striking
physical resemblance to the older woman, and she muses, "I shall
be a real comfort to me when mother's gone!" (46). Upon the
woman's death, Lucy Ann acts on this means of comforting herself,
cutting and curling her hair "into just such fashion as had framed the
older face" and replacing her own clothes and jewelry with those of
her mother (47). In doing so, Lucy Ann dramatically becomes the
"double" of her mother which nineteenth-century ideology so encouraged. Trembling with both excitement and pleasure because of
her new appearance, Lucy Ann contemplates her future in her
mother's image:

> She had dreaded her loneliness with the ache that is despair; but she was
> not lonely any more. She had been allowed to set up a little model of
> the tabernacle where she had worshiped; and, having that, she ceased to
> be afraid. To sit there, clothed in such sweet familiarity of line and likeness,
> had tightened her grasp upon the things that are. She did not seem to
> herself altogether alive, nor was her mother dead. They had been fused,

by some wonderful alchemy; and instead of being worlds apart, they were one. (47)

The mother-daughter bond makes sense of actions that might otherwise be misconstrued as twisted or delusional. Of course, Lucy Ann knows that her mother is "really" dead, just as she realizes that, despite her new appearance, she is not "really" the woman she resembles. When her looks inspire several of her young nieces and nephews to call her "grandma," Lucy Ann responds, "There! that's complete. You'll remember grandma, won't you? We mustn't ever forget her" (51). Keeping alive her mother's spirit and memory is, in fact, an act of self-assertion for this daughter.

Certainly Lucy Ann's "story" in "The Way of Peace" is the crisis of identity brought on by her mother's death, for, in losing her mother, Lucy Ann is in danger of losing the role of "daughter" so central to her selfhood. The threat of personal displacement is both illustrated and accentuated in the story through Lucy Ann's physical separation from her mother's house. Upon their mother's death, Lucy Ann's family is "terrible set ag'inst" (49) her remaining alone at the house, and they try to persuade her to give up the old place and move in with one of them. Lucy Ann refuses these offers but does agree to a protracted "visiting campaign" (52) that keeps her unhappily away from her home for months. Not knowing how strongly Lucy Ann's identity is bound up in "home," the relatives circulate Lucy Ann among themselves to "save" her from supposed solitude. However, Lucy Ann herself feels "tore up by the roots" with all this "cousinin'" (60). When she finally returns to her mother's home, she stretches her arms upward and cries, "I thank my heavenly Father!" (53).

Lucy Ann's physical transformation into Mother occurs remarkably early in the story; the rest of the tale concerns her painful separation from her home at the hands of well-meaning relations, culminating in the story's Thanksgiving Day confrontation. Pressured by her brothers' families to spend the holiday with them, Lucy Ann deceives both families so that she can quietly celebrate the day alone in her own house. Susan Koppelman asserts that this Thanksgiving Day hoax is Lucy Ann's defiance of her brothers' paternalistic control of her life, an example of a woman who "faces down the power of 'brotherly love,' or benevolent patriarchy."[51]

Koppelman's reading, however, suggests that the Thanksgiving Day plot merely reinforces Lucy Ann's earlier transformation, granting Lucy Ann opportunity to exercise her newfound status in a display of "motherly" power for the brothers and the reader. This interpretation of the Thanksgiving plot overlooks the complicity of Lucy Ann's *female* relatives in the family campaign to decide her fate. Lucy Ann's brother, John, personally sees nothing wrong with his sister living independently, but his wife Mary "thought otherwise" (50) and insists that Lucy Ann visit with them. Catching wind of the visit at Mary's home, Lucy Ann's other sister-in-law then demands equal time for her family. *Female* relatives keep Lucy Ann "cousinin'" for months at a time, and Lucy Ann's exasperation stems largely from these women's inability to recognize her independence. Upon receiving her unsolicited Thanksgiving invitation from Mary, Lucy Ann laments,

> Was she always to be subject to the tyranny of those who had set up their hearth-stones in a more enduring form? Was her home not a home merely because there were no men and children in it? (54)

While Lucy Ann's outward transformation is performed early in the story, clearly she has not been granted the *status* her mother enjoyed in the female world. The Thanksgiving Day deception thus works not so much to underscore Lucy Ann's transformation as to complete it. Her hoax is not an indictment of patriarchy but a message to women to value female bonds and define womanhood as much through daughterhood as through motherhood. Only once the daughter's right to her mother's adult status is recognized is Lucy Ann truly "transformed," and the story closes with her youngest nephew asking "Grandma" when she got well (60).

For nineteenth-century women, the mother-daughter relationship functioned to "explain" the unstated motives behind the actions of women such as Aunt Rebecca, Thamre, and Lucy Ann. The nuances of mother-daughter interaction "spoke" to women writers, and these authors in turn used this important women's relationship to bridge the gaps between women readers and the text. The power of the mother-daughter bond to bring together women from across vast distances is at the heart of Sarah Orne Jewett's "The Foreigner" (1900), a story written after *The Country of the Pointed Firs* but intended as part of the Dunnet Landing sketches.[52]

As in "On the Walpole Road," the weather ostensibly inspires the interpolated story, with the violent summer gale here reminding Mrs.

Todd "o' the night Mis' Cap'n Tolland died" (120). "The Foreigner's" frame narrator—herself a "foreigner" in the closed world of Dunnet Landing—responds to Mrs. Todd's observation, "You have never told me any ghost stories" (120). Much like this "outsider," the reader may easily be encouraged by the menacing backdrop to expect a "ghost story" and, in fact, Jewett employs several familiar ghost story conventions throughout her tale. However, the *storyteller* in "The Foreigner" never calls her tale a "ghost story" and, significantly, Mrs. Todd seems to dismiss the classification as irrelevant to the tale she has in mind:

> "Ghost stories!" she answered. "Yes, I don't know but I've heard a plenty of 'em first an' last. I was just sayin' to myself that this is like the night Mis' Cap'n Tolland died. (120)

Although overtly structured as a ghost story, "The Foreigner" upsets the expectations of the convention to spin a web of powerful, interconnected mother-daughter stories.

Mrs. Todd begins her tale by telling how Mrs. Tolland—a Frenchwoman—came to settle at Dunnet Landing, and how the woman was widowed shortly after her arrival. In relating Mrs. Tolland's tale, Mrs. Todd stresses repeatedly Mrs. Tolland's "outsider" status in the small New England community: "she come a foreigner and she went a foreigner, and never was anything but a stranger among our folks" (268). Mrs. Todd tells how the Frenchwoman made the unfortunate social mistake of dancing at a church gathering and explains how "a sight o' prejudice arose" (263), primarily among the women of the parish, because of the "awful scandal" (264). Largely ostracized by the female community, Mrs. Tolland is befriended by Mrs. Todd who nonetheless has difficulty accepting the woman's unfamiliar ways and "foreign cast" (266). Mrs. Tolland is essentially a displaced person at Dunnet Landing, someone "lost" in the world, and as Mrs. Todd later watches over the dying "foreigner," she contemplates the Frenchwoman's strange fate:

> I did think what a world it was that her an' me should have come together so, and she have nobody but Dunnet Landin' folks about her in her extremity. "You're one o' the stray ones, poor creatur," I said. (287)

The mounting details throughout the narrative of Mrs. Tolland's "foreignness" work to cast the woman in a strange, mysterious light much in keeping with "ghost story" expectations. Although Mrs. Tolland had been born in France, she was rescued by Captain Tolland in Jamaica, and her obscure past and uncertain ethnicity make her an "exotic" figure in the tiny New England town. Familiar with herbs and medicines, Mrs. Tolland would at times "act awful secret about some things," working "charms" for herself and inspiring fear in her neighbors "not to provoke her" (126). Mrs. Todd adds to this fantastic image by telling how the Frenchwoman had sensed that Captain Tolland would not return from his last voyage and by relating details of Mrs. Tolland's pagan-like celebration of her fete day.

Such details notwithstanding, Jewett deflates the growing "ghost story" suspense in the narrative by introducing familiar ghost story plot lines and repeatedly defusing them. While the others are at Mrs. Tolland's funeral, Mrs. Todd "began to hear some long notes o' dronin' from upstairs that chilled me to the bone" (130). But, of course, Mrs. Todd finds no ghastly apparition or spirit-possessed instrument, and this potential ghost story is quickly dismissed in favor of a much less fantastic episode with the wind. Later Mrs. Todd learns that she is Mrs. Tolland's sole heir and that Captain Tolland had spoken of a chest hidden somewhere in the house. But this "lost treasure" plot—along with the potential return of the drowned sea captain—likewise falls flat. No chest is ever found, and Mrs. Todd's old uncle ironically burns the Tolland place to the ground in his determined efforts to recover the "treasure." Even the climax of the interpolated story, where a ghost indeed does appear, is tellingly anticlimactic in terms of conventional ghost story expectations. Actually, the tale "o' the night Mis' Cap'n Tolland died" does not really work as a ghost story because Mrs. Todd had never intended to tell one. Instead, both Mrs. Todd and Jewett tell mother-daughter stories by carefully situating their "ghost story" within the world of mother-daughter relationships.

In telling "The Foreigner's" story, Mrs. Todd impresses on her listener Mrs. Tolland's unconnectedness, an isolation tied directly to the Frenchwoman's *motherlessness*. Significantly, Mrs. Todd again and again explains how the lonely Frenchwoman so often seemed like a child. She recalls how Mrs. Tolland was "just as light and pleasant as a child" (264) and comments how, in speaking to the woman, "You often felt as if you was dealin' with a child's mind" (271). Mrs. Tolland's childlike vulnerability touches Mrs. Todd's own mother, who senses the woman's longing for motherly affection and reaches out to her despite community prejudice. That Mrs. Tolland is longing for motherly love to ease her isolation is of course made explicit in the tale's close. Mrs. Todd tells how the Frenchwoman, just moments before her death, sat upright in her bed and "reached out both her arms" (288) toward a woman's shadowy image in the doorway: "I saw very plain while I could see; 'twas a pleasant enough face, shaped somethin' like Mis' Tolland's, and a kind of expectin' look" (288–89). The crux of both Mrs. Todd's tale and "The Foreigner" lies not so much in the apparition of Mrs. Tolland's mother as in the exchange between the two women who witness the vision. Mrs. Tolland asks her watcher—not once but twice—"You saw her, didn't you?" (289). The dying woman is not looking to validate her own impressions, for her satisfied composure after the experience indicates her certainty. Mrs. Tolland's question points to her need to know that *Mrs. Todd* saw the image too and is an appeal to Mrs. Todd's understanding as a daughter to comprehend what a mother's appearance would mean to this forlorn woman. Mrs. Todd does understand; she feels "calm then, an' lifted to somethin' different as I never was since," and she answers the dying woman, "Yes, dear, I did; you ain't never goin' to feel strange an' lonesome no more" (289).

The culmination of Mrs. Todd's story, then, is not the ghost but that moment of understanding when the "foreigner" and the New Englander truly communicate. Mrs. Todd states how Mrs. Tolland could not say more, "but we had hold of hands" (289), revealing that the two daughters had found a common language beyond words. Significantly, the Frenchwoman only becomes "real" when all the "foreign" aspects of her identity (ethnicity, speech, religion) are stripped away and she is defined as a daughter of a mother. The nineteenth-century perception of motherhood/daughterhood as an integral part of true womanhood explains what "happens" between the women in Jewett's story; neither Mrs. Todd nor the white woman reader can empathize fully with Mrs. Tolland until the "foreigner" is recast as "one of us." Through the common experience of the mother-daughter bond, Mrs. Tolland is able finally to forge for herself a place at Dunnet Landing.

The critical note of understanding voiced in Mrs. Todd's tale is echoed in the frame story as well. Like the reader, the frame narrator in Jewett's story shares Mrs. Tolland's "outsider" position in the small, tightly-knit New England community. Yet, through the mother-daughter-like bond that develops between the narrator and Mrs.

Todd (not just in "The Foreigner" but throughout the Dunnet Landing sketches), the narrator comes to feel accepted in this unfamiliar
world. As in other women's stories, the mother-daughter bond is fos-
tered through the telling of mother-daughter tales; as Mrs. Todd recounts the deathbed scene, she draws close to the narrator and says
"almost in a whisper," "I ain't told you all . . . no, I haven't spoke of
all to but very few" (285). The deathbed apparition of Mrs. Tolland's
mother is remarkable not because it is horrifically inscrutable but because it is so perfectly *fathomable* within the full context of Mrs. Todd's
storytelling. Mrs. Todd explains to her listener:

> I felt they'd gone away together. No, I wa'n't alarmed afterward; 't was just
> that one moment I couldn't live under, but I never called it beyond rea-
> son I should see the other watcher. (291)

The *naturalness* of the mother reclaiming her lost daughter subverts
the "ghost story" quality of Mrs. Todd's tale, rendering it, instead, a
"real" story in which both storyteller and her listener genuinely
believe. In confiding her "secret" mother-daughter tale, Mrs. Todd
reaffirms the mutuality of women's experience that makes her tale
possible.

The framed tale in "The Foreigner" is seemingly inspired by the
weather, for Mrs. Todd's tale "o' the night Mis' Cap'n Tolland died"
is brought on by a terrible late-August storm rattling the coast. But
before turning to Mrs. Tolland, Mrs. Todd's first thoughts are for her
own mother:

> "Oh, there!" exclaimed Mrs. Todd, as she entered. "I know nothing
> ain't ever happened out to Green Island since the world began, but I al-
> ways do worry about mother in these great gales. (250–51)

The subconscious concerns of the mother-daughter relationship are
as much a catalyst for Mrs. Todd's storytelling as is the storm. In *American Women Regionalists,* Judith Fetterly and Marjorie Pryse discuss
how Jewett's work asserts that "through generations of mothers and
mother-figures" a daughter "may retain her connection or become
reconnected with spiritual as well as cultural roots."[53] The characters
and the female reader are all "connected" through Jewett's use of the
relationship to narrow both cultural and narrative distances. Like
Mrs. Tolland, the reader too is drawn into the circle of womanhood
which women's storytelling creates.

Discussing the relationship between the woman narrator and her female reader, Judith Kegan Gardiner asserts that such works

> re-create the ambivalent experience of ego violation and mutual identification that occur between mother and daughter. The woman writer allies herself intimately with her female reader through this identification. Together they explore what is public and what is private, what they reject and what they reflect.[54]

Mother-daughter stories of the nineteenth century attest to the centrality of the mother-daughter relationship in women's lives. What has yet to be acknowledged fully is how these stories also demonstrate the importance of the mother-daughter dynamic in women's literature. As Gardiner suggests, the mother-daughter bond is a bridge that connects women readers and women's texts, allowing women to "explore" together the issues and relationships foremost in their world. The mother-daughter bond lays the foundation of connectedness that underlies nearly all of women's subsequent ties, establishing for women what Chodorow terms a "definition of self in relationship."[55] Since women-to-women ties were such a vital part of nineteenth-century women's selfhood, it stands to reason that such relationships would be employed by female artists to encode the "unsaid" details of their short fiction. In the essay "Female Sexuality," Sigmund Freud confessed that he had not really succeeded in "completely unraveling" the complex pattern of mother-daughter interaction;[56] some sixty years later, those same perplexing threads have been loosened ever so slightly, but enough to provide some insights into the intricate weave of women's lives and communication.

3

"In The Privacy of Our Own Society": Writing Female Friendship as Story

Are there no men present? Do you promise me that behind that red curtain over there the figure of Sir Chartres Biron is not concealed? We are all women, you assure me? Then I may tell you that the very next words I read were these—"Chloe liked Olivia . . ." Do not start. Do not blush. Let us admit in the privacy of our own society that these things sometimes happen. Sometimes women do like women.

—Virginia Woolf, *A Room of One's Own*

"I wish I could be with you present in the body as well as the mind & heart—I would turn your *good husband out of bed*—and snuggle into you and we would have a long talk like old times in Pine St.—I want to tell you so many things that are not *writable*. . ."

—Eliza Schlatter to Sophie DuPont, 24 August 1834

IN AN OFTEN CITED PASSAGE OF *WOMAN IN THE NINETEENTH CENTURY*, Margaret Fuller comments on the imperfect relationship between men and women within traditional marriage:

A profound thinker has said, "No married woman can represent the female world, for she belongs to her husband. The idea of Woman must be represented by a virgin." But that is the very fault of marriage, and of the present relation between the sexes, that the woman *does* belong to the man, instead of forming a whole with him. Were it otherwise, there would be no such limitations to the thought.[1]

Earlier in the work, Fuller discusses the possibility of friendship in marriage, and contends that "did [Man] believe Woman capable of friendship," he would never marry for mere convenience and enter carelessly into a union "where he might not be able to do the duty of

74

a friend" for his partner.[2] In short, in *Woman in the Nineteenth Century,* Fuller argues that true friendship between husband and wife is nearly impossible, given the unequal status of the sexes in American society.

Perhaps less familiar are Fuller's comments on the power and intensity of same-sex relationships. In an 1842 journal entry, Fuller writes,

> It is so true that a woman may be in love with a woman, and a man with a man. It is pleasant to be sure of it, because it is undoubtedly the same love that we shall feel when we are angels. . . . It is regulated by the same law as that of love between persons of different sexes, only it is purely intellectual and spiritual, unprofaned by any mixture of lower instincts, undisturbed by any need of consulting temporal interests; its law is the desire of the spirit to realize a whole, which makes it seek in another being that which it finds not in itself.[3]

Fuller goes on to recount her own friendship with Anna Barker whom she loved "with as much passion as I was then strong enough to feel." She writes of her friend, "Her face was always gleaming before me; her voice was echoing in my ear; all poetic thoughts clustered round the dear image. . . ." Fuller also says of their friendship, "This love was for me a key which unlocked many a treasure which I still possess."[4]

Fuller's description of female friendship as a "key" to otherwise unattainable "treasure" is an apt image in considering nineteenth-century middle-class women's friendship stories as well, since female friendship is, in fact, the key to understanding such stories. Fuller's own story, "Mariana," first published in *Summer on the Lakes* (1844), is particularly useful in examining nineteenth-century middle-class women's friendship stories and the ways those friendships convey "secret" meanings to women readers.[5] First, for an audience not attuned to the nuances of middle-class women's friendships, "Mariana" seems not about women's friendships at all, since the story's overt message (as presented in its closing paragraphs) addresses the problems in male-female relations in a vein similar to Fuller's remarks about marriage in *Woman in the Nineteenth Century.* In his Introduction to *The Essential Margaret Fuller,* Jeffrey Steele comments that "Mariana" serves to link women's oppression with the exploitation of Native Americans that Fuller observed while traveling out West.[6] But, if "Mariana" is primarily a story about male-female relations, then it is not an especially "good" story, since it must then be seen as structurally flawed.

Indeed, the very problems with Fuller's story suggest that a reading devoid of middle-class female-friendship considerations is largely inadequate.

Mariana is dead at the story's outset, and her old schoolmate's shock on hearing the news from Marina's aunt is the overt catalyst for the storytelling: "What I now learned of the story of this life, and what was by myself remembered, may be bound together in this slight sketch" (118). The introduction of this familiar frame device, of course, creates certain expectations in readers. Although the frame narrator states that her girlhood memories of Mariana and the aunt's story of Mariana's adult life and death will be "bound together" to become one tale, the frame device more often serves to draw attention to what lies inside the frame. Instead of being "bound together," then, the frame narrative and the enclosed narrative frequently *compete* for the reader's interest, with the framed tale becoming the "real" story to be told.

And here, certainly, lies the chief structural problem with "Mariana." Briefly, the framed story tells how a young woman's passion, creativity, and independence are smothered by the oppressions of conventional marriage. Mariana, a beautiful, free-spirited woman possessing "a touch of genius and power" (119) meets and falls in love with Sylvain, who "seemed, at first, to take her to himself, as the deep southern night might some fair star. But it proved not so" (126). The pair marry, but their union is doomed to failure: "He wanted her the head of his house; she to make her heart his home. No compromise was possible between natures of such unequal poise. . . ." (127). The couple soon fall into a familiar pattern of married existence: "Sylvain became the kind but preoccupied husband, Mariana the solitary and wretched wife" (128). Her spirit crushed, Mariana lapses into fever and dies, but not before expressing in verse her bitter disappointment and despair. "Mariana" closes with the narrator's comments on both the dead woman's poetry and life:

> It marks the defect in the position of woman that one like Mariana should have found reason to write thus. To a man of equal power, equal sincerity, no more!—many resources would have presented themselves. . . . But such women as Mariana are often lost, unless they meet some man of sufficiently great soul to prize them. . . . (131)

In light of the story's closing "moral," Fuller's sentiments on male-female relations might seem to be the crux of this narrative. But, if

"Mariana" is primarily meant to voice Fuller's ideas on husband-wife issues, why does relatively little of the narrative deal with this relationship? Well over half of the story focuses not on Mariana's relationship with Sylvain but on the female frame narrator's relationship to Mariana: her love for Mariana, her memories of their boarding school experiences, her reaction to the news of Mariana's death. Of course, the frame device itself suggests that such details be seen as "background" information leading up to the "real" story of Mariana's tragic marriage. If so, however, the sheer length of the "introductory" narrative is wholly unwarranted. It seems strange that Fuller would make her reader wait so long (a full nine pages) before introducing Sylvain into the story. Surely such "background" details could and should have been related more succinctly?

Even more tellingly, a reading centered on male-female relationships ultimately cannot explain why the frame narrator is drawing her "slight sketch" of Mariana's life. Certainly the frame narrator is a fiction to present the framed tale; nevertheless, within the reality of the short story, there must be some ostensible *reason* for the frame narrator to tell her tale. Why does the frame narrator of "Mariana" care? Do her interests lie solely in the context of Mariana's failed marriage? And, by extension, did the interests of Fuller's intended reader reside primarily in this aspect of the story?

Such questions suggest that reading "Mariana" through the lens of male-female relations is limiting, since the structural device of a female frame narrator necessarily introduces women's relationships into the story. After the opening paragraph in which the narrator establishes herself as storyteller, she moves directly to her own girlhood memories of Mariana:

> At the boarding school to which I was too early sent, a fond, a proud, and timid child, I saw among the ranks of the gay and graceful, bright or earnest girls, only one who interested my fancy or touched my young heart; and this was Mariana. (118)

Thus, the narrator "frames" her own "frame story" with the as yet untold tale of her love for Mariana, and this deeply felt emotion colors both what she personally "remembers" and "what [she] now learned" of Mariana from the dead woman's aunt. With the introduction of female friendship into the story, the frame shifts from around the marriage story to include the frame story as well, a move which warrants both the length and the weight given the narrator's "background" details.

Indeed, more than half the text deals directly with the dynamics of female friendships within the boarding school culture. When Mariana arrives at the school the other girls are at first charmed by her unconventional ways, "her love of wild dances and sudden song, her freaks of passion and of wit. She was always new, always surprising" (118). But her schoolmates soon tire of Mariana, and when the girl is daring enough to wear makeup, the others devise a cruel joke to punish "once for all, this sometimes amusing, but so often provoking nonconformist" (120). The girls don exaggerated rouge to mock Mariana, and the shock of being so abused by those "whose hearts she never had doubted" (121) sends Mariana into seizures. Above all, Mariana is devastated by the revelation that none of the girls had really been her friend:

> It was this thought which stung her so. What, not one, not a single one, in the hour of trial, to take my part, not one who refused to take part against me. Past words of love, and caresses, little heeded at the time, rose to her memory, and gave fuel to her distempered thoughts. Beyond the sense of universal perfidy, of burning resentment, she could not get. (122)

The *seriousness* with which the narrator handles the episode is telling. Surely this is no small aside, not "background" for her story, since these girlhood relationships are not presented as precursors to "real" intimacy between women and men. The narrator never doubts, never belittles, the profundity of the rouge episode, even though she did not *personally* witness it, since she had not yet arrived at the school herself. This detail, dropped casually into the storytelling, in fact proves crucial in unlocking "Mariana's" complex treasures.

Although the narrator herself had not witnessed the episode, she claims that Mariana's character was fundamentally altered by the schoolgirls' prank. Cut off from female friendship, Mariana "now hated all the world" and begins to act as an agent to destroy for others the friendship she has been denied:

> the demon rose within her, and spontaneously, without design, generally without words of positive falsehood, she became a genius of discord among them. She fanned those flames of envy and jealousy which a wise, true word from a third person will often quench forever; by a glance, or a seemingly light reply, she planted the seeds of dissension, till there was

scarce a peaceful affection or sincere intimacy in the circle where she lived. . . . (122)

Amazingly, however, the narrator states that the other girls are blind to Mariana's new character, noting that the change was largely invisible "to the *careless* observer" (122; emphasis added). Although the rouge episode has only been "whispered" to her ("the girls did not like to talk about it" [123]), the narrator construes the incident as an example of everyone's "profound stupidity" (119) in handling Mariana, evidence that the others at the boarding school are incapable of truly seeing Mariana's poetic spirit and worth.

It is precisely at this point—when Mariana is "friendless"—that the narrator enters the boarding school and is immediately attracted to the girl. Thus the rouge episode serves to prepare the reader not for Sylvain's later appearance but for the *narrator's* appearance just when Mariana "needed" her most. Here is the "story" the narrator wishes to tell, since it is the only one she actually knows—all else has been told to her by those who fail to truly appreciate their subject. The narrator feels that she alone understands Mariana and, likening the girl to the romantic heroine of Louisa Sidney Stanhope's *The Bandit's Bride* (1807), determines to provide the intimacy that Mariana's nature needs:

> Surely the Bandit's Bride had just such hair and such strange, lively ways, and such a sudden flash of the eye. The Bandit's Bride, too, was born to be "misunderstood" by all but her lover. But Mariana, I was determined, should be more fortunate, for, until her lover appeared, I myself would be the wise and delicate being who could understand her. (122)

The fact that our narrator "knows" Mariana permits her to relate not just the story behind what she hears about Mariana's life but also the "Bandit's Bride's" own deepest thoughts and feelings, even though the narrative offers no evidence that Mariana actually confided in her or even returned her affection. After weeks of unsuccessfully "courting" Mariana, the narrator finally gets on her knees and cries, "O Mariana, do let me love you, and try to love me a little" (123). But Mariana rejects this proposal, displaying a coldness which the narrator can only attribute to Mariana's continued bitterness over the rouge prank. The young lover, however, is undaunted; although the narrator feels herself "scorned" and becomes "very unhappy," she nevertheless continues to consider Mariana her "shining favorite" (123).

The narrator tells next of Mariana's reinstatement into the world of female friendship. Confronted publicly with evidence of her duplicity, Mariana again falls into seizures from which she awakens quite penitent. Too ashamed of her former deceptions to ask forgiveness, Mariana is "returned to life" (125) by a nursemaid who confides in Mariana her own tale of women's friendship:

> O my child, do not despair, do not think that one great fault can mar a whole life. Let me trust you, let me tell you the griefs of my sad life. I will tell to you, Mariana, what I never expected to impart to anyone. (124)

The nursemaid coaxes Mariana back to her circle of friends by revealing a "secret" story not of her own life, but "of shame, borne, not for herself, but for one near and dear as herself." The ironic parallel between this storytelling and the narrator's is significant. Just as the nursemaid's female friendship story "saves" Mariana, the narrator's friendship tale "redeems" Fuller's story by drawing the reader into the coterie of women who now share this heretofore untold tale of female intimacy.

Reading "Mariana" as fundamentally a female friendship story is further supported by the fact that the male-female love story which immediately follows has little meaning devoid of the narrator's girlhood "remembrances." Indeed, the narrator implies that Mariana's newfound love and trust among her boarding school friends left the girl "ready for delusion" (125) at the hands of a man. Having been momentarily restored, Mariana is abruptly summoned home and is again largely cut off from the world of female friendship when she meets and falls in love with Sylvain. The parallels between the appearances of Mariana's two lovers—Sylvain and the narrator—as well as the suitors' contrasting relationships with Mariana cast a new, more telling light on the story's closing message. True love between Mariana and Sylvain is impossible because Sylvain can never be Mariana's *friend:*

> Mariana was a very intelligent being, and she needed companionship. This she could only have with Sylvain, in the paths of passion and action. Thoughts he had none, and little delicacy of sentiment. . . . He loved to have her near him, to feel the glow and fragrance of her nature, but cared not to explore the little secret paths whence that fragrance was collected. (126)

Although she loves Sylvain, Mariana herself senses a "blank" in her communion with her husband, and soon realizes "that there was ab-

solutely a whole province of her being to which nothing in his answered" (126). That their relationship lapses so rapidly into predictable, gender-defined divisions (with Sylvain "off, continually, with
his male companions" [128] and Mariana home alone) further suggests that gender differences are at the heart of the couple's incom-
patibility. Mariana's tragic ending reveals the irony of her role as "The
Bandit's Bride," a heroine "born to be 'misunderstood' by all but her
lover." Fuller's story implies that in a gender-segregated society, such
understanding between women and men is indeed a romantic dream.

In contrast, the *narrator* understands and values Mariana's soul in
a way she firmly believes Sylvain cannot. The narrator, convinced that
she alone comprehends the full extent of Mariana's tragedy, continues to mourn her loss of Mariana even after Sylvain has recovered
from his:

> But peace be with her; she now, perhaps, has entered into a larger free-
> dom, which is knowledge. With her died a great interest in life to me.
> Since her I have never seen a Bandit's Bride. She indeed, turned out to
> be only a merchant's.—Sylvain is married again to a fair and laughing
> girl, who will not die, probably, till their marriage grows a "golden mar-
> riage." (129)

The narrator positions herself, then, not outside the story but as a
central figure in it; *she* would have proven the more adequate and appropriate "lover" for Mariana, one not distanced by the gulf of gender differences that sabotaged Mariana's marriage. In *Woman in the
Nineteenth Century*, Fuller holds the fault of marriage to be that
Woman belongs to Man "instead of forming a whole with him."[7]
"Mariana" contrasts this imperfect union with women's friendships,
underscoring the problematic nature of male-female relations by
comparing them to a love whose "law is the desire of the spirit to realize a whole."[8] The frame around the narrator's female friendship
tale closes with a poem by Mariana in which she welcomes Death to
open "her sweet white arms," for Death's heart "cannot be colder
much than man's" (129). That Death is a woman serves to complete
the narrator's opening sentiment that female friendship is the central story of women's lives.

In discussing Mariana's fateful "mistake" in marrying Sylvain,
Fuller's narrator—as is often the case in women's short stories—
addresses directly her female reader, who might find herself in a position similar to Mariana's:

Let none condemn her. Those who have not erred as fatally should
thank the guardian angel who gave them more time to prepare for judgment, but blame no children who thought at arm's length to find the
moon. (126)

By identifying her intended audience as female, the narrator reveals
that she means to share this tale of women's friendship with other
women. Fuller's story "works," then, only for a reader for whom female friendship is not only a viable but a desired (indeed, preferred)
option for true intimacy. For such a reader, "Mariana" is a story of
lost—perhaps unrequited—love and of a woman's own bitterness
over losing Mariana to one so unworthy. The constant devotion the
narrator holds for Mariana *is* the tale, lending the storytelling both
purpose and coherence, since without the female friendship there
would be no "story" at all.

Female friendships—particularly in middle-class, nineteenth-
century America—provided women artists with an ideal mechanism
for conveying meaning, because women's friendships were both so
integral to women's lives and so singular in their quality and intensity. Recent feminist scholarship has begun unlocking the treasures
of this vital female relationship. Carroll Smith-Rosenberg's study of
middle-class women's letters and diaries, "The Female World of Love
and Ritual," examines women's relationships within a cultural setting
and shows how such friendships contributed to the development of
"a specifically female world." Smith-Rosenberg argues that the "rigid
gender-role differentiation" that characterized nineteenth-century
middle-class society resulted in "sexually segregated worlds inhabited
by human beings with different values, expectations, and personali-
ties."[9] But, while women were largely excluded from the male
"sphere," they did not lack close personal relationships:

Women . . . did not form an isolated and oppressed subcategory in male
society. Their letters and diaries indicate that women's sphere had an essential integrity and dignity that grew out of women's shared experience
and mutual affection and that, despite the profound changes which affected American social structure and institutions between the 1760s and
the 1870s, retained a constancy and predictability.[10]

The existence of distinct male and female worlds meant, among
other things, that middle-class women artists could rely on an essential familiarity with the parameters of the women's sphere on the part

of female readers. Thus, important elements of the nineteenth-century female world could safely be left "unsaid" in women's short stories without compromising the stories' effect.

Along with the mother-daughter bond, women's friendships formed the basis of the "essential integrity and dignity" of middle-class women's world. Separate spheres frequently produced male-female relationships that were formal, distant, and strained; in contrast, women's relationships with each other were quite often intense, "romantic," even "sensual."[11] Smith-Rosenberg shows how nineteenth-century women friends spent many days exclusively in each other's company, slept together, kissed and embraced openly, and unashamedly expressed their love and admiration for each other in a way that twentieth-century observers would define as "lesbian" in nature. Yet, Smith-Rosenberg stresses that "intense and sometimes sensual female love" was, in the nineteenth century, "both a possible and an acceptable emotional option." The post-Freudian tendency to view same-sex relationships as fundamentally heterosexual *or* homosexual is not validly applicable to nineteenth-century, middle-class female friendships, since "romantic" love between women was both "socially acceptable and fully compatible with heterosexual marriage."[12] Of significance in considering female friendship as a structural device in short fiction is the "socially acceptable" status of such relationships. Whether or not Fuller's sentiment "that a woman may be in love with a woman" is grounded in latent homoerotic feelings is secondary to the fact that Fuller's statement reflects an approval of same-sex intimacy that was widely shared in middle-class America prior to the 1920s. Female readers would therefore *expect* women's friendships to play a part in a story such as "Mariana" which features the group dynamics of young women.

Moreover, the boarding school setting for much of Fuller's story creates the scenario for a particular form of female friendship with which many nineteenth-century middle-class women would be familiar. Nancy Sahli, in "Smashing: Women's Relationships Before the Fall," writes of the intimate, passionate love experienced between young women in colleges and boarding schools which was commonly referred to as "smashing." Sahli quotes an 1882 letter by Alice Stone Blackwell commenting on schoolgirl "smashes":

[The girls have] an extraordinary habit . . . of falling violently in love with each other, and suffering all the pangs of unrequited attachment, desperate jealousy . . . with as much energy as if one of them were a man. . . . And they write each other the wildest love-letters, & send presents, confectionery, all sorts of things, like a real courting of the Shaksperian (sic) style. If the "smash" is mutual, they monopolize each other & "spoon" continually, & sleep together & lie awake all night talking instead of going to sleep; & if it isn't mutual the unrequited one cries herself sick & endures pangs unspeakable.[13]

Certainly the narrator in Fuller's story falls for Mariana in just such a way. In recounting her unsuccessful attempts to win Mariana's favor, the narrator describes a pattern of behavior strikingly similar to the courting discussed in Blackwell's letter:

Did I offer to run and fetch her handkerchief, she was obliged to go to her room, and would rather do it herself. She did not like to have people turn over for her the leaves of the music book as she played. Did I approach my stool to her feet, she moved away, as if to give me room. The bunch of wild flowers which I timidly laid beside her plate was left there. (122–23)

Similarly, the narrator's passionate profession of love and her continued interest in Mariana despite being rejected resemble the behavior of someone utterly "smashed." Sahli shows how these schoolgirl courtships, "with a high degree of emotional, sensual, and even sexual content," were commonplace in middle-class American women's society until late in the nineteenth century.[14] Middle-class women readers knew, with very little detail, the type of relationship the narrator had hoped to share with Mariana; for such readers, the female friendship issues that pervade "Mariana" continually affect the story's tone, structure, and meaning.

In contrast, the female friendship elements of Fuller's story would likely have been less available to a popular male audience. Certainly the existence of sexually segregated spheres had many of the same implications for men's interactions as it did for women's. For example, Robert K. Martin, in "Knights-Errant and Gothic Seducers: The Representation of Male Friendship in Mid-Nineteenth-Century America," looks at the patterns of male friendship in nineteenth-century American novels and discusses how the relative exclusion of women from the male world allowed for "an enlarged . . . repertory of male friendship."[15] Martin notes how novels such as Theodore Winthrop's *John Brent* (1862) demonstrate the intensity of male friendship, since the novel's two male friends "become more than mere brothers, and rise to the level of 'complete brotherhood,' of 'knight-errantry.'"[16] Martin concludes that "the boundaries between permissible and impermissible forms of expression of male friendship were drawn very differently in mid-century American than they are now."[17]

Notwithstanding the parallel between Martin's observation and Smith-Rosenberg's remarks on women's friendships, it appears that nineteenth-century male friendship did not share the same *type* of intimacy as that of female friendship. Lillian Faderman has observed that the general acceptance of passionate female friendships in nineteenth-century, middle-class society sprang from the concept of the "asexual woman" who neither desired sex nor engaged in sexual activity unless to please her husband and to procreate; "Because there was seemingly no possibility that women would want to make love together, they were permitted a latitude of affectionate expression and demonstration. . . ."[18] However, Faderman notes that "such naivete toward same-sex love did not, of course, extend to male homosexuality" and that the very possibility of male homosexuality often limited intimacy between men.[19]

Perhaps more important, the intimacy of the male bond did not provide direct access to the nuances of women's friendships, because separate spheres rendered the very experience of friendship a gender-segregated and -defined phenomenon. Sahli cites an 1873 letter on "smashing" to the *Yale Courant,* which states, "How . . . such a custom should have come into vogue, passes masculine comprehension."[20] In contrast, Smith-Rosenberg writes that such intense female friendships made sense to middle-class women since they served for them important emotional functions:

> Within this secure and empathetic world women could share sorrows, anxieties, and joys, confident that other women had experienced similar emotions . . . [Women's troubles] were frequently troubles that apparently no man could understand.[21]

To this world of shared experience and mutual understanding, "men appear as an other or out group."[22] It is not surprising, then, that Mariana's marriage proves so lifeless since, as Smith-Rosenberg contends, middle-class marriage in nineteenth-century America often meant living "with a person who was, in essence, a member of an alien group."[23] What women shared—distinct from the "alien" under-standing of men—is the key to "Mariana."

Many scholars have noted, however, that what women share in friendship has long been absent in literature. Louise Bernikow, in *Among Women*, contends that women's friendships are missing from the male-dominated canon because women converse among them-selves in a "code" that men cannot translate:

> Perhaps Prufrock is the problem. If he cannot hear what the mermaids say or if they do not in fact sing to him, he cannot tell us. In the same way, Nick Carraway the narrator in *The Great Gatsby*, can observe women talk-ing with one another but offer no report on what they say because he is not part of the conversation. The absence of female intimacy in literature is, partially, the result of the masculine point of view. Many of our stories are told by narrators who have no part in the conversation.[24]

Through the "masculine point of view," women are shown primarily in their relationships with men; women's ties with each other are, at best, secondary. Faderman cites *The Friendships of Women* (1868) by William Alger as an example of the nineteenth-century attitude that female friendships served merely to occupy young women until their more "serious" relationships with husbands, and suggests that such trivializing of female friendship accounted for the broad acceptance of female intimacy (such as that in "Mariana") as fundamentally "harmless."[25]

Similarly, Susan Koppelman comments on the belittling of women's friendship experiences within the patriarchy:

> If what appears to be a friendship supports the status quo—that is, rein-forces the power of the patriarchy—it is socially recognized and valuable. If the friendship enables two women to survive hard lives in the patriarchy without giving out, up, or in before their usefulness has ended, it is an in-visible but permitted relationship.[26]

Further, Tess Cosslett contends that female friendships are "invisible" in literature but abound in women's personal correspondence be-cause women's friendship experiences have long been deemed un-worthy subjects for fiction:

> Here, I think, the important point is what is considered as suitable mate-rial for a *narrative* as opposed to a letter: what counts as an event in a story.

The world of women's friendships seems to be perceived as something *static,* outside the action that makes a story. In narrative, men are thought to be needed to create tensions and initiate significant action.[27]

But, clearly, many nineteenth-century women artists did not feel this way, since (as in "Mariana") their fiction at times ironically juxtaposes the "significant action" between men and women with the "invisible," but often more meaningful, dynamics of female friendship.

"What makes a story" is central to the narrative structure of Elizabeth Stuart Phelps's "At Bay" (1867).[28] As in "Mariana," the woman narrator device sets up a tension between the love story that is "told" and the female friendship story that is overtly "untold." "At Bay" frames the female narrator's "frame" with a familiar nineteenth-century fictional device, the Editor's Note, which here serves to draw the reader's attention away from the story young Sarah will tell and to the storytelling itself:

[I had intended to tell the story myself; but the young woman's account is so much more to the point than another could be that I send her MS just as it fell into my hands, only premising that it seems to me worth the reading. E.] (19)

The "story" young Sarah apparently means to tell is a fairly cliched romantic drama. Orphaned and penniless, Martie Saunders is forced to find work and lodgings in the cold, uncaring city. She secures a position, but is soon hounded by the unscrupulous Job Rice, who promises to seek vengeance when she scorns his marriage proposals. Job spreads malicious rumors about Martie's virtue, which costs her most of her friends, her place at the boardinghouse, and nearly her position. Helpless against Job's lies, Martie gives in and agrees to marry her antagonist, only to renounce Job publicly at the altar. Martie is rescued from the furious Job by Davie Bent who had loved and believed in her all along. The couple marry, and their story ends with Martie and Davie living "happily ever after."

The story Sarah relates is, perhaps, more "successful" than the one told by "Mariana's" narrator, both in terms of structure and outcome; Sarah's tale comes complete with suspenseful plot twists, long-suffering lovers, a clear villain, and a happy ending. Indeed, the very *predictability* of "At Bay's" fairy tale romance works to distract the reader's interests away from that plot and toward the less directly told story of Sarah's place in the above melodrama. Throughout "At Bay," the romantic love story is continually interrupted—at times, even overshadowed—by the "real" story of female friendship that Sarah inadvertently tells. Ostensibly, Sarah wishes to tell Martie's story because of its "story-like" quality—"It used to seem like a story to me as it went along" (19)—but this reason for the narrative is immediately contradicted by the female friendship context Sarah offers for her storytelling: "It is nothing of a story after all, when you come to it; so very simple and short. I suppose it means more to me because she *was* Martie" (20). In effect, Sarah is telling two stories here: the easily recognizable "story" of male-female relationships and the much less apparent "non-story" of her own relationship with Martie and the feelings she has for the girl throughout *their* ordeal.

Sarah herself has left home to find work in the city, so she immediately feels for and is attracted to the newly arrived Martie:

> The night that she came to our house—I boarded with Mrs. M'Cracken— I thought that she had the most homesick face I ever say. . . . Mrs. M'Cracken asked, Would I let her sleep with me for a night or two? I don't generally like to sleep with strangers, but I had the queerest feeling about her, as if I wanted to talk away or kiss away that homesickness out of her face; so I said Yes most willingly. (21)

Sarah loves Martie almost immediately, and the girls' feelings for each other are expressed through the kind of physical intimacy so common in nineteenth-century women's interaction:

> I only kissed her, that was all. After I was in bed and the lamp was out, and we had lain still a while, I only stooped over and kissed her softly on both her eyes.
>
> I was afraid she would be angry with me, but I really could not help it. And instead of being angry with me what do you suppose she did? Why, she threw her arms about my neck and broke out crying. . . . (23)

The two quickly become inseparable, living and working together and vacationing together at Sarah's family's farm. Significantly, Sarah stands by Martie throughout her ordeal with Job Rice, despite the obvious threat to her own reputation that her continued friendship poses. When Martie is turned out of Mrs. M'Cracken's house, Sarah alone loudly protests in her friend's defense, and when Martie finds lodgings elsewhere, Sarah insists on moving in with her:

As to its "hurting my character," which [Martie] argued in her dear, un-selfish love, I said, as I had said about my respectability, I would make my own or I would go without. (33)

The intensity of Sarah's feelings for Martie and Sarah's need to tell *her* story in the process of telling Martie's is, of course, what the "Editor" had sensed from the outset as what makes Sarah's narrative "worth the reading." Just as the interpolated romance plot is only a "story" to Sarah "because she *was* Martie," Sarah's narrative is a story to the Editor because of *Sarah.* The Editor, then, becomes the frame narrator who validates Sarah's feelings and her status as a central fig-ure in Martie's experience by "not narrating" and instead granting Sarah her own voice. Phelps's layered storytelling creates an inter-esting dynamic between the frame narrator (the Editor) and the framed narrator (Sarah) in "At Bay." Immediately following the Edi-tor's comment that Sarah's account "is so much more to the point than another could be," Sarah begins her tale:

> I will tell you about it as well as I can, *since you ask me to;* though it fright-ens me to think of showing it to any one who knows how to write books; and I do hope you will excuse all mistakes and remember that I can't tell things in a fine way, but only as they happened. Of course you will not have it printed as it is, but will write it out yourself, and fix it up in some pretty way. (19; emphasis added)

That the Editor has somehow elicited the tale from Sarah suggests an understanding between the Editor and the storyteller that is crucial in shaping the narrative, since Sarah continues to address the Editor directly throughout her tale. When telling how she kissed Martie's eyes on their first night together, Sarah states, "I believe you would have done just what I did if you had been there" (23). Similarly, in re-lating how a boy at the family's farm fell for Martie, Sarah exclaims, "well, well! poor fellow—I don't mind telling *you*—I am afraid Dan thought a great deal of Martie . . ." (27; emphasis Phelps's). Such im-plied confidence between Sarah and the Editor suggests that the Ed-itor is a woman, which would explain why Sarah entrusts her with the cherished Martie story in the first place. It also suggests that, despite Sarah's self-depreciating remarks and her comment that the Editor will "fix up" the story "in some pretty way," Sarah believes that the Ed-itor can appreciate *her* story and that the Editor will not, in fact, write

Sarah out of Martie's life. The tacit understanding between Sarah and the Editor thus ensures that the female friendship story gets told both to the Editor and to the reader.

Louise Bernikow has noted how, regardless of the social "acceptability" of female ties such as that shared by Sarah and Martie, female friendship represents an inherent challenge to patriarchal order; "In friendship, women do for each other what culture expects them to do for men and in that way, female friendships are subversive."[29] The subversiveness in female friendship extends to its use as a narrative device as well. In "At Bay," Phelps employs the female friendship elements of her story to counter—and, ultimately, to explode—the conventional fairy tale romance plot. The subversiveness of Sarah's narrative is evident in Sarah's ambivalence toward Martie's participation in male-female relations. Sarah recounts how, upon first seeing Martie, she admired the girl's fine features and states, "I wish I had been the only one that noticed; yet not exactly that either, come to think of it" (22). Similarly, Sarah initially denies Job Rice's request to meet Martie, although she cannot explain why she does so. At Martie's wedding to Job, Sarah notes the unhappiness of Martie's other lover:

> Davie Bent was there, trying to flirt a little with Sue. He was very white. I felt sorry for Davie; sorrier than I did for Martie, or for—well, no matter who! (35)

Sarah seems equally "sorry" when Martie finally marries Davie:

> I think it was the sweetest, stillest wedding that I ever saw. I think it made me very happy—at least—yes, I think it did. (36)

And, of course, the story closes with Sarah's tear stains on the paper countering her claim that she feels good in her loneliness to think at times of "Davie's wife" (37).

Sarah's uncertain feelings about Martie's "happily ever after," coupled with her willingness to risk her own reputation for Martie's sake, have led critics such as Koppelman to suggest a "lesbian" reading of "At Bay," calling it "a story of unrequited, sacrificial, romantic love rather than a friendship story."[30] Such a broad distinction between female "love" and "friendship," however, is not useful in a nineteenth-century context where the parameters of such relations so often converged. Instead, the emotional necessity of deeply committed women's ties can be seen as the source of Sarah's ambivalence. Mar-

tie's assimilation into the world of heterosexual relationships represents a profound loss for Sarah, the pain of which is only com-
pounded by Sarah's own spinster fate. Carol Farley Kessler calls Sarah
and Martie's story a "quieter, losing story of friendship between two
young women" that emerges "between the lines" of the narrative.[31]
Indeed, much like "Mariana," "At Bay" is intended at least partly to
show the tragedy of lost female ties due to the demands of patriarchy.
In both stories, however, the usurpation of the reader's interests by
the female friendship plots works to undermine the "losing" status of
the female-centered stories. By giving the friendship stories not
merely a voice but one that can overpower the familiar tones of the
romance convention, the women's friendship plots prove more com-
pelling—more "real"—for women readers than do the tragic or
happy male-female stories. Thus, for nineteenth-century women
readers, stories such as "At Bay" and "Mariana" create a space where
women's relationships can "win" despite the obstacles they may face
in other contexts. "At Bay" challenges conventional notions of what
makes a story by having the reader become emotionally engaged not
in the overt romance plot but in the more "covert" friendship story.

In Alice Cary's "Charlotte Ryan" (1853), the narrator's relationship
to the story's central figure proves much more ambiguous than that
shared between the storytellers and their subjects/friends in "At Bay"
and "Mariana."[32] Like Phelps and Fuller, Cary uses the frame narrator
device, the at times detached female observer who "sketches" Clovernook life throughout Cary's work. However, "Charlotte Ryan's" narrator is far more distant—both in relation to the narrative action and to
Charlotte herself—than are the more directly "involved" women in the
other stories, and such "distance" fundamentally informs the female
friendship stories within and outside the narrative frame.

Charlotte Ryan is the simple but beautiful daughter of Clovernook's "last family" (105), and her rustic farm existence affords little
opportunity for her to experience life. Indeed, upon observing Charlotte in her dingy surroundings, the narrator cannot help wishing
that Charlotte might find some position "better suited to her capac-
ities and inclinations" (108). This wish seems almost magically
granted when an unexpected letter summons Charlotte to the "fantasy" home of well-off relations:

> Of course Charlotte had heard much of her uncle, Captain Bailey,
> and his daughters, and in childish simplicity supposed them to be not

only the grandest but also the most excellent people in the world. They dwelt in her thoughts on a plane of being so much above her, that she involuntarily looked up to them and reverenced them as if they were of a fairer and purer world. . . . Nobody about Clovernook was at all comparable to them in any respect, as they lived in the beautiful region of her dreams. (109)

The "fairy tale" of Charlotte's rise from Clovernook's "last family" to a position in Captain Bailey's house is abruptly replaced by another familiar fairy tale scenario, that of Cinderella. Charlotte is asked to come and teach her two cousins the domestic skills needed to handle the family's newly acquired farm. But the two spoiled, selfish girls are far too used to their pampered city customs to take to chores, and Charlotte is quickly saddled with all the household cares. Moreover, the cruel condescension of these "evil stepsisters" toward the unrefined Charlotte works to make her painfully ashamed of herself and quite miserable:

> In education, in knowledge of the world, in the fashionable modes of dress, the Misses Bailey were in the advance of her, as much as she, in good sense, natural refinement, and instinctive perceptions of fitness, was superior to them. But unfortunately she could see much more clearly their advantages than her own. Falling back on the deficiencies of which she was so painfully aware, she could not think it possible that she possessed any advantage whatever, much less any personal charms. (115–16)

In this strained, class-conscious environment, Charlotte and her cousins are scarcely friends, since the Bailey girls consider Charlotte "a country cousin, whom father has taken a fancy to patronize" (117).

Upon this unhappy scene arrives Sully Dinsmore the "Handsome Prince" who traditionally carries Cinderella away from her persecutors. The reader soon discovers, however, that Sully is just as self-centered and insidious as are Charlotte's cousins, for he greatly enjoys toying with the beautiful but unsophisticated farm girl's affections. Instead of rescuing Charlotte from her misery, Sully worsens her situation, since his careless flirtations with all three girls spark new jealousy and competition between them:

> From that day the cousins began to be more and more apart; the slight disposition to please and be pleased, which had on both sides been struggling for an existence, died, and did not revive again. (130)

Charlotte is initially comforted by her naive belief that Sully loves her. However, her dreams of "happily ever after" with her lover are dashed when Sully thoughtlessly misses a date, leaving Charlotte waiting at the appointed spot for hours. Realizing that she has meant nothing to either Sully or her cousins, Charlotte is brought to the lowest, most unhappy point in her life, and she determines to leave her "*rich* friends" and return home in the morning:

> This decision made, she undressed and went to bed, as usual, and tried to compose herself to sleep by thinking that she was about as ugly and ill-bred, and unfortunate in every way, as she could be; that everybody disliked and despised her, and that all who were connected with her were ashamed of her. (133)

From this dismal state, Charlotte is "rescued" not by a Handsome Prince but by a beautiful young woman. Sully misses his rendezvous with Charlotte because he is preoccupied with a new arrival, Louise Herbert, with whom he is still flirting when Charlotte returns from her futile wait in the woods. Miss Herbert therefore overhears Charlotte's heartbreakingly earnest "Why did you not come?" and she immediately understands the situation at hand:

> when she saw Charlotte, and heard the trembling inquiry, and the answer of indifference, she read the little history, which to the young girl was so much, and appreciating, so far as she might, her sorrows, determined to win her love . . . (135)

As with the young women in "At Bay," Louise reaches out to Charlotte in a familiar nineteenth-century scene for female intimacy—the shared bed. Ostensibly sleeping with Charlotte to save her hosts trouble, Louise seeks to win the girl's heart through a kindness manifested in physical tenderness:

> "How cold you are," she said, creeping close to her companion and putting her arm around her. Charlotte said nothing, and gave a hitch, which she meant to be from , but, somehow, it was toward the little woman. "Oh, you are quite in a chill," she added, giving her an embrace . . . (134)

Louise insists on wrapping Charlotte's chilled feet in her own petticoat, and the two young women fall asleep in each other's arms.

Ultimately winning Charlotte's love, Louise is the wealthy "Hand-

some Prince" who carries away Charlotte. It is significant that Louise
befriends Charlotte because of her tacit understanding of another
woman's suffering, requiring only the subtlest clues to "read the little history" and comprehend Charlotte's ordeal. Such understanding
makes it much more credible—at least initially—that a woman would
identify with Charlotte and bridge the distances between them than
would a man such as Sully Dinsmore. However, this new version of
"happily ever after" is itself undercut by the ever-present frame device, in particular, by the relationship between the frame narrator
and Charlotte. From the outset, the frame narrator draws attention
to her *distance* from Charlotte, introducing the girl first and foremost
as part of a family "a little behind everybody else at Clovernook"
(105). Such class difference is underscored by the narrator's opening observation that Charlotte could, "under the hands of an artist,"
be transformed into a girl who would do well "in society" (108). Thus
the narrator's initial wish that poor Charlotte somehow be granted a
better position in life reveals her true desire to see the farm girl ele-
vated to her *own* position, one where real connection—perhaps even
friendship—is more possible.

By the story's close, this wish seems to have become reality; the
narrator tells us that a year or two after Charlotte's rescue "changes
and chances brought me for a moment within the circle in which she
moved as the admired star" (136). Together "socially" for apparently
the first time, the narrator congratulates Charlotte on her "new position" (137), only to have the socialite burst into uncontrollable
tears:

> "What would mother think, if she saw me here, and thus? . . . And dear lit-
> tle Willie and sturdy Jonathan. . . . I suppose they sleep in their little nar-
> row bed under the rafters yet, and I—I—would I not feel more shame
> than joy if they were to come in here to-night! Oh, I wish I had staid at
> home and helped mother spin, and read the sermon to father when the
> weekly paper came . . . (137)

This closing confessional scene in which the narrator learns her folly
reveals the "fairy tale" quality of Louise and Charlotte's relationship,
for, despite her dramatic "rescue" by her female admirer, Charlotte
remains a *friendless* girl throughout the story. Although Charlotte and
Louise love each other, their relationship is viable only if Charlotte is
willing to uproot, transform, and finally deny her selfhood. Unlike
Fuller's "Mariana," "Charlotte Ryan" speaks to the at times ambigu-

ous power of female friendship to offset the superficiality of male-female relations. Charlotte has found one to love her, but their intimacy is possible only if Charlotte "steps up," and the frame narrator's
closing remarks on the foolishness of her initial aspirations for Charlotte suggest that a *true* friend would not have wished something "better" for the farm girl.

Without the frame narrator and her "failed" friendship with
Charlotte, Cary's story merely replaces one fairy tale romance with
another. The female friendship frame thus renders "Charlotte Ryan"
much more accessible and believable to Cary's reader by pulling the
Louise Herbert plot out of the realm of fantasy. In the end, Charlotte
Ryan does not live "happily ever after"; instead, she remains friendless and alone.

The Lowell Offering's "Ann and Myself: No Fiction" (1841) represents a working-class women's story in which such class issues shape
women's friendships and friendship tales.[33] The title's assurance that
what follows is "no fiction" is obviously intended to lend believability
to the tale. But for whom? Unlike such stories as "Mariana" and
"Charlotte Ryan," the works in *The Lowell Offering* consciously addressed a dual audience: the mill girls who allegedly produced and
read the *Offering* and a middle-class audience whom the *Offering*
sought to impress with its exhibition of the "mind among the spindles." "Ann and Myself" tells how and why "Matilda" became a factory
girl, relating her desire for agreeable working conditions and "satis-
factory" (194) pay which was doubtless shared by most mill girl readers. The title's assurance that the story is "true" was therefore quite
likely intended for the *Offering*'s "outside" readers who were less
familiar with (and, in fact, prejudiced against) mill girls and factory
life. Nonetheless, such middle-class readers were familiar with
women's friendships in fiction, and "Ann and Myself" uses this familiarity to court both the ear and the understanding of its middle-
class audience.

Friends from childhood, Matilda and Ann remain close despite
the three-month separation when each becomes a "school ma'am."
The teaching term over, Matilda accepts an invitation to visit friends
in New Hampshire, "although [she] had no favorable opinion of factory places, and more especially of factory girls" (193). Despite her
misgivings, Matilda is so impressed by the discreet and "civilized"
(194) manners of the factory girls that she becomes one herself. Convincing Ann to join her, the two live "in uninterrupted friendship"

(195), using their increased wages to advance their education in ways
that would have been far out of reach for mere "school ma'ams."

When a family emergency calls Ann home, however, Matilda is
stunned:

> The intelligence was painful to Ann, but doubly so to me—for while I
> sympathized sincerely with her in affliction, my heart could not bear the
> thought of an uncertain separation. (195)

Ann stays at home well past the family's crisis, and Matilda's sorrow
increases when she gets word of Ann's upcoming wedding: "The idea
of a rival was more than I could endure" (195). The intensity of the
narrator's love for Ann and the woman's grief over losing her friend
to a "rival" lover echo notes played in many middle-class women's
friendship stories. But, in "Ann and Myself," there is an important difference from the scenario shown in a story such as "Mariana." Matilda
is pained to give up her friend, "Yet I could not reproach [Ann] for
I had reason to believe her affianced husband was worthy her choice"
(195). While Matilda will sorely miss Ann, her narrative suggests neither bitterness toward her friend's husband (as in "Mariana") nor ambivalence about Ann's happiness (as in "At Bay").

In "Ann and Myself," marriage is not the divisive force that in-
trudes upon female friendship; instead, unjust middle-class prejudice
against factory girls proves the real threat to women's intimacy. Now
enjoying "a competency of this world's goods" (195), the married
Ann whispers to her newly arrived friend, "You must be 'school
ma'am' while you are here, for factory girls are nothing thought of
in this place" (195–96). Matilda goes along but cannot long endure
the "bondage" of the charade and soon returns to "where I could enjoy a dearly-loved freedom" (196). Unlike the pitiful narrator in
Phelps's story, who is left behind in lonely spinsterhood, the narrator
in "Ann and Myself" deliberately turns away from her friend, vowing
never again to be "the dupe of false opinions" (196).

In this way, "Ann and Myself's" working-class narrator positions
herself *above* the now middle-class Ann in terms of fidelity and true
friendship, a plot theme which, no doubt, played well with the factory girls who read the *Offering*. Perhaps more significantly, however,
the story's closing betrayal surely resonated for a middle-class audience accustomed to reading women's friendship stories. By positioning her indictment of middle-class bias within a female friendship

context, the narrator is able to make her tale "real" for an audience who would otherwise view itself outside/above the mill girl experience. The *friendship* renders "Ann and Myself" "no fiction" for this reader, meshing the women's friendship issues with the story's class messages and social agenda. *The Lowell Offering* and the dynamics of the mill girl culture will be discussed in more detail in the following chapter on women's communities and community stories.

The theme of female friendship transforming women—usually, but not always for the better—surfaces time and again in nineteenth-century women's short stories. In 1897, Sarah Orne Jewett spoke of the dramatic impact friends have on one's life even after they have parted, stating: "There is something transfiguring in the best of friendship."[34] This sentiment, of course, plays prominently in Jewett's 1888 women's friendship story, "Miss Tempy's Watchers."[35] Yet, as this story shows, women's friendships (like the mother-daughter bond) also served as a means for nineteenth-century writers to redefine dramatic "action" in the short story.

As in mother-daughter stories such as Freeman's "On the Walpole Road," many female friendship stories are characterized by a deliberate absence of "action," a notable sense that little overtly "happens" in the tale. The epitome of such "actionless" stories, "Miss Tempy's Watchers" presents a scene that is typically characterized by inactivity and outright boredom. Indeed, any "action" in watching over the dead is largely atypical, the result of something unexpected, outlandish, mysterious, romantic, comic, tragic. Nothing like this happens in "Miss Tempy's Watchers," however; Mrs. Crowe and Miss Binson quietly pass the night talking and sewing, and the two big "events" of the evening—a midnight snack and a check on the body—are remarkably uneventful:

In the silence . . . the fact of their presence in a house of death grew more clear than before. There was something disturbing in the noise of a mouse gnawing at the dry boards of a closet wall near by. Both the watchers looked up anxiously at the clock; it was almost the middle of the night, and the whole world seemed to have left them alone with their solemn duty. (46)

The very *stillness* of the scene, the slowing down of time to accentuate the weariness of the watchers' vigil, invites the reader to reconsider the possibilities of "movement" in a story.

Tempy's two watchers are cast initially as strikingly different in

temperament, status, and circumstance. Although Mrs. Crowe is re-
spected and well-off, she is a "stingy woman" when it comes to giving
to others (41). On the other hand, Miss Binson is a poor spinster
whose difficult life caring for her widowed sister's family is still "brim-
ful of pleasure to herself" (41). Apparently all these women share is
their role as Miss Tempy's "oldest friends," a fact that seems to have
done little to bring them together in the past. Yet the very act of
watching works to minimize all that separates the women by emphasizing their common distinction as "friend" (the story's title itself
defining the women through their relationship to Tempy). The two
watchers soon begin to share a confidence inspired by the inherent
intimacy of their situation:

> Each had already told the other more than one fact that she had deter-
> mined to keep secret; they were again and again tempted into statements
> that either would have found impossible by daylight. (41)

The sharing between Mrs. Crowe and Miss Binson is not just the action in the story; it proves to be the very motivation for the action, the
reason these women are selected by Miss Tempy to be her watchers:

> They were both old schoolmates and friends of Temperance Dent, who
> had asked them, one day, not long before she died, if they would not come
> together and look after the house, and manage everything, when she was
> gone. She may have had some hope that they might become closer friends
> in this period of intimate partnership, and that the richer woman might
> better understand the burdens of the poorer. (42)

The watchers do "come together," in part through their shared
sense that Miss Tempy is somehow still there with them. After the two
go upstairs to check on the body, Miss Binson says, "I don't know why
it is, but I feel as near again to Tempy down here as I do up there. . . .
I feel as if the air was full of her, kind of" (46). Moreover, the women
both feel "that they were being watched themselves," "as if there were
a third person listening" to their talk (42). Certainly this "third person listening" plays a crucial role in Jewett's story. Through the benevolent influence of the third "watcher," Mrs. Crowe and Miss Binson
gain "new sympathy" (49) for each other; by continuing even after
death to "watch" over her friends, Miss Tempy demonstrates the
power of friendship to "transfigure" women.

But the key to what makes Jewett's story work is the scene which closes out the night, one which is, ironically, even more "uneventful" than the scenes before it. After viewing the body and eating a light meal, the two women fall asleep and the story comes seemingly to a complete standstill:

> Overhead, the pale shape of Tempy Dent, the outworn body of that generous, loving-hearted, simple soul, slept on also in its white raiment. Perhaps Tempy herself stood near, and saw her own life and its surroundings with new understanding. Perhaps she herself was the only watcher. (49)

By pairing the scene where the watchers view the body with one in which the two women themselves fall asleep, the focus—and the action—shifts from watching to *being watched*. And, while Miss Tempy is the "watcher" within the story, the reader, of course, occupies a parallel position in relation to Miss Binson and Mrs. Crowe. By slowing down time and capturing the taxing weariness of watching, Jewett's story reconstructs the notion of plot "movement" to include motionlessness. Jewett's masterful scene of Miss Tempy "watching" encourages the reader both to identify with the dead woman and to engage in precisely the same action she performs. Through such mirroring, Tempy's priorities become the reader's; Miss Tempy had brought her two oldest friends together so that they can become friends, and the reader is there not merely as witness but as participant in the event by recognizing female friendship *as* action.

Other examples of women's stories in which friendship is all that "happens" are Alice Brown's "Joint Owners in Spain" (1895) and Lydia Maria Child's "The Neighbour-in-Law" (1846).[36] In Brown's story, the two most disagreeable residents at the old ladies' home find a way to cohabit peacefully by drawing a chalk line and occupying separate "houses" in their shared quarters. Friendship becomes possible through the women's shared sentiments that "Folks don't want to be under each other's noses all the time" (65) and that each woman needs to "have somethin' that's [her] own" (63). In "The Neighbour-in-Law," Mrs. Fairweather is able to break down the fences surrounding old Hetty Turnpenny's affections, despite Hetty's deliberate efforts to be distant, petty, and troublesome. What is most striking in Child's story is the astonishing patience and persistence of Mrs. Fairweather in her campaign to befriend Hetty. When Hetty tries to vex her neighbor by sweeping dirt onto the walk, Mrs. Fairweather smilingly has the front swept and holds no grudge. Susan Koppelman comments on the apparent illogicality of the women's friendship:

When we say that there is a reason for a friendship to begin we are acknowledging an ulterior motive or a practical concern perhaps being
joined to a spontaneous emotional response that, when examined, results
in a feeling that this new friendship "makes sense." In "The Neighbour-
in-Law" there is neither a reason for the friendship nor a spontaneous
emotional attraction between the two women. It is the utter "apractical-
ity," the complete absence of any of the usual motivations, that makes this
story of the beginning of a friendship between two women so unusual. . . .[37]

The same "apractical" element characterizes the friendship in "Joint
Owners in Spain," since both women have obviously lived without befriending their various roommates for years. The overt "senselessness"
of the friendships in these stories forces the reader to reconsider the
true purpose of such ties and to discover the relationships' underlying meaning both to the characters and to the stories themselves.

Of course, "loving thy neighbor" is a standard tenet of Christian
piety, and befriending another (particularly one who does not immediately reciprocate the kindness) is considered spiritually en-
nobling. Indeed, Carolyn L. Karcher notes how Mrs. Fairweather's
saintly patience in "The Neighbour-in-Law" reflects the Quaker ethic
of "good-humored friendliness."[38] However, a traditional Christian
reading of the friendships established in Brown's and Child's stories
fails to recognize any profit in such "senseless" friendships outside of
the women's moral gain, and is thus wholly in line with conventional
male representations of women's relationships. Faderman describes
the "sentimental pictures" of women friends drawn by men in nineteenth-century literature: "Two sweet females uplifting each other
morally, but ultimately entirely dependent on men whether depend-
ence brought them joy of tragedy."[39]

Smith-Rosenberg suggests that the world of women's relationships provided an atmosphere for much more than spiritual uplift:

This was . . . a female world in which hostility and criticism of other women
were discouraged, and thus a milieu in which women could develop a
sense of inner security and self-esteem. . . . They valued each other.
Women, who had little status or power in the larger world of male concerns, possessed status and power in the lives and worlds of other women.[40]

Similarly, Nancy Cott, in *The Bonds of Womanhood*, comments how
nineteenth-century middle-class women highly valued their female

friendships because they represented "relations between equals," as opposed to the hierarchical relations between women and men.[41] Thus, in forming female friendships, women also built for themselves avenues to self-esteem, personal growth and identity, and community status. Faderman writes of male artists' failure to depict "what women writers who lived the experience themselves could depict," namely how female friendship gave women the "strength and encouragement to achieve in the world."[42]

This unstated motive for friendship among women is surely behind the puzzling friendships in Brown's and Child's stories. In devising their plan to live as friendly "neighbors" in their shared room, the two old women in "Joint Owners in Spain" regain the privacy and dignity they had long been denied in institutional living. Likewise, in "The Neighbour-in-Law," Mrs. Fairweather gains praise and admiration from women neighbors for the "miracle" she performs on Hetty Turnpenny (14). Of course, the happy outcome of both stories is never really in doubt from the outset. But the "unsaid" story of personal gain through friendship lends credibility to such seemingly implausible relationships and explains why establishing friendships would be the focus of so many middle-class women's stories.

The strength and self-esteem derived from women's friendships also "makes sense" of the tremendous personal sacrifices that are often a part of nineteenth-century women's friendship tales. For example, in Edith Wharton's "Friends" (1900), Penelope Bent allows her friend Vexilla Thurber to take over the position at the local school even though Penelope wants the job back.[43] There is certainly an element of charity in Penelope's act. Her marriage plans having fallen through, Penelope needs to return to teaching in order to support herself and her mother, as well as to rebuild the savings lost in the aborted wedding trip. But Vexilla's situation seems much more desperate (if not more pitiful), since Vexilla must support "a helpless grandmother, a crippled brother and an idle sister" (75) through underpaid tutoring and typing jobs. Penelope's former position represents a unique opportunity for Vexilla to advance and gain security.

The willingness to sacrifice is not merely one-sided, however. When Penelope leaves to be married, Vexilla agrees to replace her friend on the condition that she be permitted to resign should Penelope return: "She's a devoted friend," explains a schoolboard member in revealing the situation (79). True to her word, Vexilla expresses no resentment upon Penelope's return, and even attempts to

spare Penelope's feelings by downplaying her own desire for the
position:

> And there's another thing I want to tell you right off, Penelope! I
> know just what you are—always thinking of other people first and your-
> self last; and I don't want you to think it's any loss to me to—to give up
> that place. I don't want to keep it, Penelope! It's a relief to me to give it
> up. I never should have got used to it. I'm not half bright enough, any-
> way! I don't much believe they'd have kept me more than one term, even
> if—and it doesn't suit me, somehow! I'd rather go back to my old work.
> I—I think I'd have resigned, anyway. I'm sure I would, Penelope! (87)

At this point, the dramatic tension in "Friends" seems to focus on
which woman will "lose" or, more specifically, which woman will per-
mit the other to "lose." Casting Penelope's decision solely in terms of
loss, however, overlooks all that Penelope gains, above and beyond
the moral "uplift," in giving Vexilla the job. Having been abandoned
in Louisville by her fiancé, Penelope returns home broken and hu-
miliated. Too ashamed to tell even her own mother of her ordeal,
Penelope suffers a tremendous blow to her self-esteem which strips
her of her identity:

> Every line of the furniture, every twist in the pattern of the wallpaper,
> seemed to repeat the same "I know thee not!" No, she was not the Pene-
> lope Bent who had lived there through so many happy, monotonous
> years; she was a stranger who had never been in the room before, and who
> knew as little of its history as it knew of hers. (81)

Penelope's uncertainty renders her sad and distrustful, as is evident
in her initial bitterness upon learning of Vexilla's appointment. But
Vexilla's sincere love and concern, and her eagerness to give the job
back to her friend, work to restore Penelope's faith in others and herself. Penelope's male lover deserts her, but her female lover proves
true, and Vexilla's loyalty gives Penelope strength to leave her hometown altogether and start life over in New York:

> Her step had lost all hesitancy. She seemed to be moving with decision to-
> ward a definitely chosen goal. In the course of the past hour her whole re-
> lation to life had changed. The experience of the last weeks had flung her
> out of her orbit, whirling her though dread spaces of moral darkness and
> bewilderment. She seemed to have lost her connection with the general

scheme of things. . . . Now the old sense of security had returned. . . . [S]he had escaped from the falling ruins and stood safe, outside herself, in touch once more with the common troubles of her kind . . . (91)

In sacrificing her job, Penelope ironically regains her "position" through the reaffirmation of her place in other women's lives. Leah Hackleman observes that Penelope's sacrifice "does not make her a martyr," since her act allows her to move forward in life allied with other women.[44] By acknowledging and valuing her identity as "friend," Penelope becomes "herself" again, a self that is inextricably bound up in female ties. Her movement from victim to victor demonstrates, in Hackleman's words, "the transforming power of female friendship."[45] It also demonstrates how women writers "transformed" the definition of movement in a story, shifting the focus from the more obvious action in the story (Penelope's abandonment by her male lover) to the less overt action of female friendship. Whether the sacrifice involves a job, as in Wharton's story, or a man, as in Mary Wilkins Freeman's "Friend of My Heart" (1913),[46] the act of self-sacrifice "makes sense" to women readers who understand the dignity and self-empowerment in such acts. In this sense, women's friendship stories offset the view that such personal sacrifices are "the figment of the shallowest sentimentality," as William Dean Howells maintains in *The Rise of Silas Lapham* (1885).[47]

Perhaps Jewett's "Martha's Lady" (1897) best demonstrates the need to "read" female friendships in nineteenth-century women's stories, since "Martha's Lady" brings together many of the characteristics of middle-class female friendship stories already noted.[48] As in Wharton's story, "Martha's Lady" presents friendship as the force behind women's determination to overcome adversity and to succeed. Harriet Pyne's beautiful and graceful niece, Helena, is considered "a young lady of . . . opportunities" (525). In contrast, Miss Pyne's young servant, Martha, is plain and "ungainly" (525) and so slow to learn her new duties that she is in danger of losing her position. Despite these differences, Helena takes a liking to Martha and soon helps her understand "by a word and a quick touch the right way to do something that had gone wrong and been impossible to understand the night before" (525). Helena's small assistance and kindness speak volumes to Martha, who senses that the pretty and refined house guest is "a friend after all." Martha's budding feelings take full bloom when she overhears Helena defending Martha's skills to Miss Pyne:

From that moment, [Martha] not only knew what love was like, but she knew love's dear ambitions. To have come from a stony hill-farm and a bare small wooden house was like a cave-dweller's coming to make a permanent home in an art museum; such had seemed the elaborateness and elegance of Miss Pyne's fashion of life, and Martha's simple brain was slow enough in its processes and recognitions. But with this sympathetic ally and defender, this exquisite Miss Helena who believed in her, all difficulties appeared to vanish. (526)

Helena's friendship "transforms" Martha, inspiring her to improve herself and become a more capable maid. "All for love's sake" (527), Martha learns the finer arts of domestic care and in the process overcomes the loneliness and hopelessness that had been daunting her. Helena's friendship grants Martha both the ability and the desire to succeed, and Martha tells Helena, "It was you made me think I could ever learn" (528).

The intensity of Martha's love also demonstrates the potential "subversiveness" of female friendship, in terms of both male-female relationships and traditional plot structures. Much like Sarah in "At Bay," the female lover in "Martha's Lady" promises her love to Helena and proves true to this pledge for more than forty years. Although her friend is long gone—Helena marries and moves still farther away, to Europe—Martha continues to live her life "trying to please one whom she truly loved" (528) and forever considering in her daily routine "whether this thing would please [Helena], or that be likely to fall in with her fancy or ideas of fitness" (531). Eternally patient and devoted, Martha faithfully awaits Helena's long-promised return like Penelope waiting for Odysseus. Helena herself seems almost "heroic" in Martha's mind, becoming Martha's "idol," her "perfect friend," an ideal "which grew at last to be like a saint's vision, a heavenly figure painted upon the sky" (528). As in "Charlotte Ryan," the "savior" who rescues the poor farm girl from her misery is a woman, but here the less fortunate girl is sincerely grateful for what friendship has done to her, and the story's closing message is intended to be much less ambivalent. "Love conquers all" in "Martha's Lady" and the tale ends with Helena returning after her long absence, and Martha's loyalty finally rewarded with a familiar bedroom embrace:

"You have always remembered, haven't you, Martha dear?" [Helena] said. "Won't you please kiss me good-night?" (533)

While the centrality of female friendship to Jewett's plot and the subversive elements of its woman "hero" structure may well have appealed to Jewett's audience, it is also important to consider how "Martha's Lady" functions as a *middle-class* women's story. Interestingly, all that "happens" in "Martha's Lady" takes place very early in the story; Helena's direct contact with Martha is, in fact, quite brief and occurs when both women are young. Except for the closing reunion scene, the rest of Jewett's story chronicles Martha's forty-year wait for Helena's return, with both Martha and the reader hearing secondhand the events of Helena's busy married life abroad. But for Martha, this "other" Helena is largely unreal and has little bearing on Martha's image of her, as evidenced by Martha's genuine shock when the returning Helena shows the signs of her forty-year absence:

"Oh, my Miss Helena is an old woman like me!" and Martha gave a pitiful sob; she had never dreamed it could be like this; this was the one thing she could not bear. (533)

In her decades-long vigil, Martha becomes frozen in time, with Jewett's narrative emphasizing how Martha's life "grew more and more monotonous" (531) as the years creep by. Nonetheless, Martha's outwardly meaningless life bears a real but secret meaning for her, because "everyday, as she had promised, she thought of Miss Helena" (531). Thus, Martha's love for Helena—framed by her actual interaction with the other woman—*becomes* the story, and this interpolated story is achieved by Jewett (as in "Miss Tempy's Watchers") slowing down time and stripping away all other "action" in the tale. The story of Martha's wait becomes a tableau vivant of female friendship, "actionless" only to those who do not recognize what the scene is intended to convey.

"Martha's Lady" works, then, for the reader who, like Martha, reads both meaning and purpose into the story's apparent "void." Indeed, for Martha, the "real" events in life become irrelevant as she deliberately denies the significance of Helena's "other" life: "These things seemed far away and vague, as if they belonged to a story and not to life itself; the true links with the past were quite different" (531). By downplaying the relevance of what traditionally makes a "story," "Martha's Lady" underscores the importance of the "true links" of female friendship that comprise "life itself." Martha tells no one of her love for Helena, and to an "outsider" her life seems empty;

indeed, "nobody's life could seem duller *to those who could not under-stand*" (528; emphasis added). The critical need to understand Martha's life in the context of her female friendship is expressed by Jewett herself in a letter to her friend, Sarah Whitman. Commenting on Martha's "dull" life, Jewett says, "I thought that most of us had be-gun to grow in just such a way as she did, and so could read joyfully between the lines of her plain story. . . ."[49]

Glenda Hobbs has noted that Jewett's reference to how "most of us grow" reflects the belief that

> most adolescent women learn about caring from a "best" friend of the same sex. We need to read "between the lines," or to recall our own mem-ories to appreciate the intensity of Martha's attachment to Helena.[50]

Equally important, Jewett's comments also reveal that her anticipated audience is primarily female.

In the same letter to Sarah Whitman, Jewett speaks directly of the "unsaid" elements of female friendship at work in "Martha's Lady":

> but it is those *unwritable* things that the story holds in its heart, if it has any, that make the true soul of it, and these *must be understood*, and yet how many a story goes lame for lack of that understanding . . . (emphasis added)[51]

Indeed, without prior conviction that Martha not only could but *should* love Helena so intensely, Martha's life appears sadly pathetic and Jewett's story slow and inane. And, significantly, the "unwritten" relationship issues that make "Martha's Lady" possible for Jewett's reader were most likely tied to the middle-class status of the intended audience. Perhaps the notion of a servant girl falling in love with her mistress and offering a lifetime of dutiful service because of that love was an appealing tale to the mistresses who read *The Atlantic Monthly*. Although the story suggests that Helena cares for Martha, too, and grants her small remembrances, the narrative's focus is on Martha's near dog-like devotion to her long absent mistress, and Jewett's story carefully maintains the neatly drawn class lines within the relation-ship. For example, while Helena remembers to invite Martha to her wedding, the older and wiser Cousin Harriet knows it is "most im-prudent and girlish to have thought of such a thing" since Martha "would be out of her element" (530). Martha—who never learns of the invitation—must settle for a piece of cake and Helena's handkerchief, which becomes a sacred relic in Martha's scant collection of valuables. Further, when Helena finally does return, the mistress-servant relationship is never wholly usurped by friendship; the story closes with Martha once more waiting on "her lady" and Helena granting the servant permission to kiss her goodnight.

In "Charlotte Ryan," the class dynamics tied to female friendship worked to undercut the "fairy tale" elements of Charlotte's rescue. "Martha's Lady," however, reads much more like a middle-class female friendship fairy tale in which—like Sleeping Beauty—the completely dependent woman waits in suspended animation for her beloved to set her back into "action" (with a kiss, no less). In "Martha's Lady," female friendship can bridge any distance except social ones, since the very definition of "friendship," on which the story depends, is based on nineteenth-century middle-class ideology. Jewett's story, then, is viable only if its female friendship is "believable" as well.

Noting the relative absence of female friendship in men's literature, Virginia Woolf, in *A Room of One's Own,* comments that in such an omission "so much has been left out, unattempted."[52] Woolf contrasts this sense of something "missing" with the excitement and possibility in encountering "Mary Carmichael's" story about women friends:

> That is a sight that has never been seen since the world began, I exclaimed. And I watched, too, very curiously. For I wanted to see how Mary Carmichael set to work to catch those unrecorded gestures, those unsaid or half-said words, which form themselves, no more palpably than the shadows of moths on the ceiling, when women are alone, unlit by the capricious and coloured light of the other sex.[53]

While the story of nineteenth-century middle-class women's friendship must speak this "unsaid" language of "women alone," it must also relate how, by the turn of the century, such language had begun to change. With the popularization of psychological theories on latent or repressed sexual motives and desires, women's emotional and physical intimacy (which had earlier been so freely expressed) increasingly became "suspect" and taboo. Faderman says of the shift in social attitudes:

> Perhaps love between women was permitted to flourish unchecked in the nineteenth century because the fact of the New Woman and her revolu-

tionary potential for forming a permanent bond with another woman had not yet been widely impressed upon the popular imagination, as after World War I when New Women emerged in great numbers. It was then that love between women came to be generally feared in America and England. The emotional and sensual exchanges between women, which correspondence and fiction tell us were a common form of affectional expression for centuries, suddenly took on the character of perversion.[54]

The fear of female companionship as a chosen substitute for marriage (and not a compensatory consequence of spinsterhood) is expressed even earlier, as in an 1898 *Ladies Home Journal* article, "The Intense Friendships of Girls," which decries young women's "so-called ecstatic friendships."[55] In particular, the writer condemns the tendency of "the ecstatic girl lover" to be satisfied with the affections of her friend exclusive of any interest in men: "To my mind there is something wrong about such a woman." The writer likewise voices her distaste for the physical manifestations of "ecstatic" friendships such as "a rapturous kiss" or "a close embrace"; "Bad manners, my dear girls, bad manners!" In a similar vein, the "latent" sexuality of female intimacy can be seen in Kate Chopin's 1895 short story "The Falling in Love of Fedora," in which Fedora's unacknowledged passion for a younger man is expressed in her "long, penetrating kiss" upon the mouth of his look-alike sister.[56] As the subversive potential of female intimacy became increasingly threatening, women artists were often constrained in their representation of women's love. Surely, Jewett's 1908 comments to Willa Cather, concerning Cather's adoption of a male persona in "On the Gull's Road," reflect the sexual "divide" that progressively separated the women and the writing of Jewett's and Cather's generations:

> The lover is as well done as he could be when a woman writes in the man's character,—it must always, I believe, be something of a masquerade. I think it is safer to write about him as you did about the others, and not try to be he! And you could almost have done it as yourself—a woman could love her in the same protecting way—a woman could even care enough to wish to take her away from such a life, by some means or another.[57]

Apparently for Cather and her audience, the "masquerade" of male-female intimacy was "safer" than the love Jewett describes.

As contemporary readers we too are distanced from Jewett's sentiments in a way that is unavoidable and not wholly reparable. It is

simply not possible for a post-Freudian audience to refrain from allowing psychological and pseudo-psychological conceptions of gender relations, sexuality, and gender identity to enter into our reading
of texts and thus to intrude on the intimacy presumably shared between nineteenth-century middle-class women writers and their intended readers. Smith-Rosenberg states that "the long-lived, intimate, loving friendship between two women" is one aspect of
nineteenth-century female experience "which consciously or unconsciously we have chosen to ignore."[58] No doubt, twentieth-century
difficulties in dealing with the dynamics of nineteenth-century
women's relationships have contributed to the "marginalization" of
many women's friendship stories.

Nevertheless, the very act of acknowledging these previously ignored relationships and stories begins to bridge the cultural distances and invites women readers to recognize what we share and can
identify with in nineteenth-century friendship tales. For example,
Nancy Chodorow suggests that the social construction of parenting
and motherhood creates in women "complex relational needs"[59] that
cannot be fully satisfied in ties with men: "One way that women ful-
fill these needs is through the creation and maintenance of important personal relations with other women."[60] Similarly, Luise Eichenbaum and Susie Orbach comment on the fundamental role female
friendship still plays in the lives of women:

> For many women, intimate relationships with women, friends, sisters,
> aunts, and co-workers are a bedrock of stability in their lives. The emo-
> tional texture of women's friendship is woven into the fabric of their daily
> lives. Indeed *a woman without a best friend is a very lonely woman.* There is an
> exquisite intimacy of female friendship, the sharing of experience, of dar-
> ing, of pain, of challenge. (emphasis Eichenbaum and Orbach's)[61]

While nineteenth-century middle-class female friendship is dis-
tinctive in its manifestations, there remains a common bond of
emotional interdependence in women's lives that serves to make
such "distant" female friendships potentially accessible to "other"
women.

Janice G. Raymond observes how the conventional view of
women existing solely in relation to men "has consistently perceived
women together as women alone."[62] However, nineteenth-century
women's friendship stories reveal how "women alone" in fact share
in an entire world of powerful relationships long hidden from "out-

side" eyes. Margaret Fuller prized her female friendship as the "key" to unlocking "many a treasure." Similarly, in valuing the role of female friendship in nineteenth-century women's stories, we too unlock the secret "treasure" of friendship that made women's lives and stories so rich.

4

Picking Up "Other Women's Destinies": Nineteenth-Century Women's Community Stories

And in that country the women love to sit and talk together of summer nights, on the balconies, in their vague, loose, white garments,—men are not balcony sitters,—with their sleeping children within easy hearing, the stars breaking the cool darkness. . . . Experiences, reminiscences, episodes, picked up as only women know how to pick them up from other women's lives,—or other women's destinies, as they prefer to call them,— and told as only women know how to relate them . . .

—Grace Elizabeth King, "The Balcony" 1892

Thine in the bonds of womanhood.
—Sarah M. Grimke

IN *COMMUNITIES OF WOMEN: AN IDEA IN FICTION*, NINA AUERBACH writes, "The unformulated miracle of the community of women is its ability to create itself."[1] The image of women living in "community" is especially relevant to viewing nineteenth-century American women, particularly middle-class women. Scholars such as Carroll Smith-Rosenberg and Barbara Welter have noted how separate spheres and "the cult of true womanhood" worked to shape nineteenth-century women's world, to forefront women's identities as women and to define the parameters of appropriate middle-class female existence.[2] Common roles as wives, mothers, daughters, aunts, sisters, and the relatively similar—and limited—range of experience such roles allowed, gave rise among many nineteenth-century middle-class women to a sense of shared lives, natures, values, and destinies. Nancy Cott writes:

Women practicing the domestic vocation perceived it as an experience that united them with other women. The canon of domesticity made motherhood a social and political role that also defined women as a class, and became the prism through which all expectations of and prescriptions for women were refracted. . . . Furthermore, evangelical Christianity's championing of the spirit over the flesh, together with its reliance on a female constituency, insinuated the idea that women's moral nature overcame the physical, freeing them from carnal passion. Though that notion . . . has frequently been interpreted as oppressive to women, it not only implied women's moral superiority but also created proud solidarity among women. . . .[3]

The various forms of female "solidarity," of course, came to have many and far-reaching social and political implications in nineteenth-century America; but the "unformulated miracle" of women's communities had an impact on women's short fiction as well. Women's sense of community—the awareness of themselves as inhabitants of one half of a fundamentally gender-segregated world—influenced not only women's stories but the very means by which their stories were told.

Sandra Zagarell identifies the emergence of a "narrative of community" in early nineteenth-century American literature and notes that "at least initially, its main practitioners were white women of the middle classes."[4] Beginning with the extremely popular village sketch, Zagarell traces the development of a "community" genre that positions the self "as part of the interdependent network of the community rather than as an individualistic unit,"[5] contending that community fiction "postulates a relationship between women's culture and writing that is also structural."[6] Although Zagarell discusses the impact of community-building on storytelling, she does not address how "unsaid" understanding ultimately constructs both communities and community stories. For example, in discussing the narrator in Sarah Orne Jewett's *The Country of the Pointed Firs* (1896), Zagarell takes note of the delicate balance between the speaker's "insider" empathy and "outsider" analysis.[7] However, beginning with Mary E. Wilkins Freeman's "A Church Mouse" (1891), we shall see that these insider/outsider positions (as well as the ways that they become blurred) themselves result from the unsaid meanings that inform storytelling. "A Church Mouse" is an especially good example of a nineteenth-century women's community story, since it presents the "miracle" of a female community "creating itself" and of the writer using the female community as a device to tell her tale.

In "A Church Mouse," the poor, displaced Hetty Fifield sets up house in a corner of the village meetinghouse despite the initial objections of town leaders.[8] All goes well for Hetty, who keeps the meetinghouse in spotless perfection, until the congregation is offended one Sunday by the smell of Hetty's boiled cabbage. There is a general consensus that Hetty must go, but before she can be ousted Hetty bolts the door, creating a standoff between herself and the growing crowd of villagers who threaten to break down the door. In the story's climax, Hetty appears in the gallery window and pleads her case to the crowd, not only convincing them to let her stay but gaining for herself a private room for her possessions. "A Church Mouse" closes with Hetty's establishment in her new home and her triumphant ringing of the church bells on Christmas day.

The structure of Freeman's story inevitably draws our attention to the pivotal "gallery window" scene, where Hetty is able to fend off the proposed violence against herself and the meetinghouse door. Freeman, however, prepares her reader for this final showdown through a series of confrontations that carefully foreshadow the crisis and its outcome. "A Church Mouse" opens with the verbal sparring match between Hetty and Deacon Gale over Hetty's desire to take over the sexton's job, and this initial confrontation is soon followed by the scene where the minister, Gale, and another deacon confront Hetty over setting up house in the church gallery. In both early confrontations, Hetty deftly deflects the objections of opponents to her plans largely because the men can offer no alternative. Alone and penniless, Hetty genuinely has nowhere to go, and the churchmen are hard-pressed to respond to her demand: "I dun' know where I'm goin'; mebbe I can go to your house?" (410). But, while these initial confrontations basically fizzle out without resolution, the reader is prepared for a more eventful one with the warning "All that time a storm brewed; then it broke . . . " (413).

Notwithstanding such an ominous tone, we soon know that an acceptable outcome to Hetty's situation will be found, for the narrator tells us as much midway through the story: "It was three months from the time Hetty took up her abode in the church, and a week before Christmas, when the problem was solved. Hetty herself precipitated the solution" (417). Significantly, the narrator offers this assurance

just before to the final confrontation between Hetty and the selectmen. Deacon Gale and the other churchmen inform Hetty that a new
home has been arranged for her with Mrs. Radway, and Hetty, "small
and trembling and helpless before them," responds "like a little animal driven from its cover, for whom there is nothing left but desperate warfare":

> "You ain't goin' to take me to that woman's!"
> "You'd be real comfortable—"
> "I ain't goin'."
> "Now, why not, I'd like to know?"
> "I don't like Susan Radway, hain't never liked her, an' I ain't goin' to
> live with her." (419)

The stalemate between Hetty and the churchmen brings on the promised "storm" that soon ensues in which Hetty locks the meetinghouse
doors and holds off her pursuers. However, the narrator has likewise
promised a "solution" to the Hetty problem, and this assures the reader
all along that, in fact, Hetty will *not* be forced to live with "that woman."
By prefacing the story's central action with the promise that the situation will be resolved satisfactorily, the narrator actually encourages the
reader to disregard the "solution" offered by the selectmen and look
for some more suitable answer to the crisis. Indeed, much like the
churchmen themselves, the reader cannot really envision anyone drag-
ging the old woman by force out of her makeshift home.

At an apparent deadlock in negotiations, Deacon Gale brightens;
"I'll go over an' git mother. . . . Mother'll know how to manage her"
(421). And here, of course, is the "solution" the narrator has promised. At first, Mrs. Gale comes fully prepared to join the townsmen's
efforts to remove Hetty, "fiercely" (421) beating on the locked door
and demanding to be let in. But as the crowd grows mob-like and becomes increasingly bent on besieging Hetty's "sacred castle" (422)
with a crowbar, the women begin to side with Hetty or, more directly,
to side against the violence their husbands propose:

> "They are a parcel of fools to do such a thing," said Caleb Gale's wife
> to another woman. "Spoil that good door! They'd better leave the poor
> thing alone till to-morrow. I dun' know what's goin' to be done with her
> when they git in. I ain't goin' to have father draggin' her over to Mis' Rad-
> way's by the hair of her head.
> "That's jest what I say," returned the other woman. (423)

When Deacon Gale decides that Mother will know better how to "manage" Hetty, he voices the belief that Mrs. Gale, at some level, understands Hetty better than the churchmen, that his wife has something in common with Hetty that might prove useful in swaying the old woman.

What Hetty and the other women *share* becomes more pressing as the crowd builds, culminating in the pivotal gallery window scene. While the overall structure of Freeman's story highlights this scene, an examination of Hetty's speech—what she literally *says* from the window—does little to explain how Hetty is able to turn the tide of public opinion and, in the end, save her home. Trembling with fear and excitement, she says:

> I jest want to say a word. . . . Can't I stay here, nohow? It don't seem as if I could go to Mis' Radway's. I ain't nothin' again' her. I s'pose she's a good woman, but she's used to havin' her own way, and I've been livin' all my life with them that was, an' now I'm gittin' too old for't. If I can jest stay here in the meetin'-house, I won't ask for nothin' any better. . . . Won't you let me stay? I ain't complainin' but I've always had a dretful hard time; seems as if now I might take a little comfort the last of it, if I could stay here. I can't go to Mis' Radway's nohow. (424)

While surely heartrending, the pitiful tenor of Hefty's speech cannot alone account for the story's reversal, since Hetty had earlier made much the same appeal to the village leaders, to no avail. If Hetty cannot convince these listeners to let her stay at the meetinghouse despite her humble pleas and pathetic demeanor, how, then, is she able to win the crowd with her appeal from the gallery window? In other words, if her speech is essentially the same, what is different in Hetty's confrontations with the selectmen and her confrontation with the crowd that leads to such contrasting outcomes?

Of course, the "difference" lies in Hetty's audience. In the scene just prior to Hetty's speech, the townswomen engage in a subtle but definite "coming together" in which they distance themselves from the men and the violence the men threaten. As the crowd outside the meetinghouse moves toward action, the wives' collective alliance shifts, in part because of the women's exclusion from the male-directed decision-making process:

> Mrs. Gale went up to Caleb and nudged him. "Don't let them break that door down, father," said she.

"Well, well, we'll see," Caleb replied. He moved away a little; his wife's voice had been drowned out lately by a masculine clamor, and he took advantage of it. (423)

With the introduction of other women into the story's final confrontation, "A Church Mouse" changes both thematically and structurally for, much like Deacon Gale, Freeman relies on women knowing what transpires among women to "manage"—or structure—her tale.

Ann Romines asserts that when the townswomen hear Hetty's speech, "they are stung, by sympathy, into alliance and action."[9] Romines' statement, however, implies that the men in the crowd are largely without "sympathy" for Hetty, a judgment that is unfair and untrue. The men in "A Church Mouse" are not persuaded by Hetty's speech because, on a fundamental level, they really do not *hear* it. Indeed, the story opens on the issue of "hearing," with Caleb Gale's dismissal of Hetty's desire to be sexton: "I never heard of a woman's bein' saxton" (407). In this opening scene, Mr. Gale repeatedly refuses to listen to Hetty, telling her, "There ain't no sense in such talk" (409), "I ain't goin' to stop to hear such talk" (409), "Don't you see it ain't no use talkin' such nonsense" (410). Similarly, Gale will not hear Hetty's reasons for not wanting to live with Mrs. Radway, telling Hetty, "You hadn't ought to speak that way about her" (420).

In contrast, when Hetty begs to say "jest one word" to the crowd, Mrs. Gale calls out: "Say all you want to, Hetty, an' don't be afraid" (424). The townswomen do, indeed, "hear" Hetty's speech, and respond not merely with sympathy but with understanding. When Hetty explains, "I can't go to Mis' Radway's nohow," Mrs. Gale's response both acknowledges and validates Hetty's reasoning: "You sha'n't go one step to Mis' Radway's; you couldn't live a day with her" (424). The women in the crowd "hear" the unexpressed motives behind Hetty's refusal—the difficulty in living with another woman "used to havin' her own way," the indignity of never having one's own home—because such motives echo the domestic lives and values these village women share. The townswomen understand Hetty's plight because their common experiences as housewives allow them to hear Hetty's real reasons for wanting to live at the meetinghouse instead of the ostensibly more "comfortable" home of Susan Radway. Thus, "A Church Mouse" pivots on the tacit understanding between village housekeepers which unites Hetty with the women in the crowd and induces the townswomen to take up Hetty's cause. Once conscious of Hetty's true hardship, Mrs. Gale largely shames the men in the crowd into letting Hetty stay, twice saying "I should laugh if she couldn't" (424). Although Hetty tells essentially the same story to both "audiences," her appeal simply does not speak to the selectmen in the same way it does to the townswomen.

Many critics have remarked that "A Church Mouse" presents the phenomenon of the female community "creating itself"; for example, Romines notes how the townswomen "recognize their community" with Hetty, and Paul Lauter writes how Hetty's passive resistance against male authority "mobilizes the support of the women of the community."[10] Of equal importance, however, the sense of "community" that is the crux of the story is also a key structural device in the work. The reader is methodically led to the climactic "meetinghouse" scene, only to be left to decide for herself what actually transpires in the confrontation. The story itself provides no immediate explanation; there is no reason given for the townswomen's "conversion," no narrative commentary as to whether such a reversal is particularly exceptional, reasonable, or believable. Clearly, Freeman assumes that her audience *knows* what happens between the women in the crowd and the woman in the gallery window, since she leaves such critical information (which, in essence, *is* the story in "A Church Mouse") primarily "unsaid." Thus, in presupposing that the critical reversal in her story will "speak" to her audience, Freeman is relying on the same shared understanding that underlies the dramatic turn of events in the tale. "A Church Mouse" is a women's community story on two levels, since the acknowledgment and appreciation of the village women's domestic values are immediate and complete only when the readers themselves share those same values. In reading Freeman's community story and deciphering "what happens," nineteenth-century women were themselves invited to share in the "unformulated miracle" of women overcoming differences and recognizing their common lives. The dramatic reversal in Hetty's fate is most "believable" to a reader who both comprehends and is convinced by the crowd's otherwise inexplicable change of heart.

As we have seen, the mother-daughter relationship and women's intimate friendships were vital parts of nineteenth-century women's lives. As Caroll Smith-Rosenberg observes, however, women who shared in such close relationships "did not form isolated dyads but were normally part of highly integrated networks" of women.[11] Similarly, Nancy Cott explains that the continuity of experience across generations that characterized such networks contributed to "women's construction of a sex-group identity"[12] which worked to further reinforce women's ties:

> Women's reliance on each other to confirm their values embodied a new kind of group consciousness, one which could develop a political consciousness. The "woman question" and the women's rights movement of the nineteenth century were predicated on the appearance of women as a discrete class and on the concomitant group-consciousness of sisterhood.[13]

Recent feminist criticism has noted how housekeeping and the domestic sphere served both to unite women and to inform their fiction with the language of the female community. For example, Helen Fiddyment Levy in *Fiction of the Home Place* notes how such writers as Sarah Orne Jewett, Willa Cather, and Ellen Glasgow employ the domestic sphere to counter—and challenge—dominant male values and male versions of the "American" experience. Focusing on shared female expression, Levy states that these women writers "seek a language vibrant with emotion, which reflects women's communal experience and past history as a remedy for the impersonal elaborate public speech that values differentiation and innovation—in a word, separation."[14] Similarly, Romines demonstrates how the assumption of a housekeeping "sisterhood" influenced the shape of nineteenth-century domestic fiction:

> the story of housekeeping, the "home plot" of domestic ritual, has generated forms and continuities very different from those of the patriarchal American canon and pushes readers to attend to texts that are not inscribed in conventionally literary language. Domestic language often seems invisible to those who have not learned to read it.[15]

Surely "A Church Mouse" presupposes middle-class women's collective "ear" for such domestic language.

The act of making women's domestic language public—of turning "non-literary" discourse into "literature"—posed a special challenge to nineteenth-century women writing about women's experiences. Some women's stories address this dilemma by, in essence, speaking a double language in which conventional devices are used to frame women's "unconventional" community stories. In Harriet

Prescott Spofford's "Circumstance" (1860), for instance, readers may readily recognize the story's "Divine Providence" design and conceptualize the tale within a larger Christian/Puritan tradition in American fiction.[16] Pounced on by a cougar (known to the settlers as an "Indian Devil"), a young wife holds off death by placating the animal with song. The woman's husband follows her voice and finds his wife in the cougar's jaws, but is able to get off a shot and kill the beast. The woman is saved from one "Indian Devil" only to discover that both she and her small family have unwittingly been delivered from another as well; in an ironic closing "twist" (so essential to nineteenth-century plot conventions), the family returns home and finds that their night-long adventure in the woods has spared them from the Indian massacre that has left their settlement in ashes. "Circumstance" closes on a moralistic note, echoing Milton in describing the young couple's struggles ahead: "For the rest,—the world was all before them, where to choose" (92).

While the story's sensational plot and white Christian perspective clearly are meant to appeal to a large middle-class audience, the source of the tale's real power lies elsewhere. Spofford moves beyond the limits of her romantic plot and moralistic message by centering the tale on the wife's ordeal in the forest. Thelma J. Shinn observes that "Circumstance" is "startlingly unusual" in its realistic portrayal of the incident: "a very real wife and mother draws on the art of her life—the hymns and lullabies and folk tunes she has sung—to placate a wild beast and defend herself against death."[17] Indeed, the very crux of the tale is how the woman is able both to appease the cougar and to sustain herself spiritually and emotionally throughout her torturous experience; the ironic plot twist at the story's close truly pales in comparison to the account of the woman's psychological ordeal. In making this "real" episode the heart of the tale, Spofford invites her readers to look more carefully at the art both the young woman and Spofford herself use, an art tied directly to women's collective voice and experience.

As Shinn has observed, the realism of "Circumstance" is achieved through a striking juxtaposition of the ordinary and the extraordinary. Realizing that only song can save her now, the frantic young wife unconsciously begins her night-long recital with "the cradle-song with which she rocked her baby," and even as she sings she wonders, "[H]ow could she sing that?" Spofford's story, of course, provides the answer:

And then she remembered the baby sleeping rosily on the long sette before the fire,—the father cleaning his gun, with one foot on the green
wooden rundle,—the merry light from the chimney dancing out and
through the room, on the rafters of the ceiling with their tassels of onions
and herbs, on the log walls painted with lichens and festooned with ap-
ples, on the king's-arm slung across the shelf with the old pirate's-cutlass,
on the snow-pile of the bed, and on the great brass clock . . . (85)

Given the young woman's real life, what else *would* she sing, even under such fantastic conditions? The songs the young woman calls on to
hold the cougar at bay—lullabies, square dances, psalms, folk bal-
lads—are indeed a catalogue of rural domestic life, and her choice of
tunes no doubt seemed quite "natural" to Spofford's female readers.

Of interest here is the way the subtle progression in the woman's
songs reveals her mental movements, and how this shaped the story
for middle-class women readers. Significantly, the focus of Spofford's
story shifts at a pivotal point in the narrative from psychological realism to a more conventionally structured plot. "Circumstance" gives
voice to women's domestic lives and values, but at a key point in the
narrative this voice becomes strangely silent. Alone and just inches
from death, the wife knows that her voice is her only support, "that
with her voice ceased her existence!" (87). But, as she is fully exer-
cising her voice's power to "bewitch" its listener, the woman's husband and child arrive, and here seems to end the story of female communication and community. With the introduction of the device that
will precipitate the traditional "rescue" scene, the wife loses hold of
the spiritual ecstasy that had at that point upheld her and looks instead to her husband to deliver her:

her face contracted, growing small and pinched; her voice was hoarse and
sharp,—every tone cut like a knife,—the notes became heavy to lift,—
withheld by some hostile pressure,—impossible. One gasp, a convulsive
effort, and there was silence,—she had lost her voice. (91)

The spell snapped, "Circumstance" seems to become a fairly typical
adventure story once more: the husband's crack shot saves the day,
and the frame around the wife's mental ordeal closes with the final
twist of God's inscrutable Providence. But *why* does the wife lose her
voice at such a crucial point in the narrative? And how does this overt
break in the story's psychological realism relate to the female-centered themes and values that shape the tale up until that point?

A careful examination of the young wife's catalogue of songs reveals a telling progression in her mental wanderings which denotes not a break but *continuity* in both the story's meaning and its structure. For, although the wife's lost voice might appear to be a device to introduce the more "plotted" adventure story of the family's rescue, actually it is much in keeping with the psychological realism Spofford achieves throughout. The young wife, in fact, loses her voice at several key points earlier in the evening. She begins her night's singing with a cradle song, but the thought of home and family that subconsciously accompany the tune so overwhelm the singer that it "made a sob of her breath, and she ceased" (85). The cougar immediately resumes its attack, so the woman turns successively to "a wild sea song" (85), "the gayest reel that ever answered a fiddle-bow" (85), a "tune of a hornpipe" (86), and "an Irish jig" (86). Such familiar community songs, however, serve only to lead the young wife's thoughts back to home and husband; "If there were yet any tremor in the tone, it was not fear . . . it was nothing but the thought of the log-house and of what might be passing within it" (86). Her mind distracted once more by the images of her family, the woman again stops singing and is subsequently bitten by her captor. Of course, the woman would sing anything that kept the cougar at bay; but the "anything" that comes to her mind is inextricably tied to her domestic existence and her roles as wife and mother.

The female community's influence on the young wife's voice is further suggested by the repeated association between her art and the traditionally female art of witchcraft. When she finds that singing the same song over and over irritates the cougar, the wife decides to "vary the spell" (86), and in doing so "charm[s]" (87) him into a trance-like state:

> as she suddenly flung up her voice again, he steeled himself composedly on the bough, still clasping her with invincible pressure to his rough, ravenous breast, and listening in a fascination to the sad, strange U-la-lu that now moaned forth in loud, hollow tones above him. He half closed his eyes, and sleepily reopened and shut them again. (86)

The ties between the wife's voice and the female community are again evidenced in the "spell" the singing casts over the woman herself. Singing melancholy songs of sorrow, the wife wonders why her husband has not searched for her and feels that he has "failed her" (87).

The wife then unconsciously turns to the songs that most directly link her to the women's community; "and without being aware of it, her voice forsook the songs of suffering and sorrow for old Covenant hymns,—hymns with which her mother had lulled her" (87). Her mother's voice echoing in her own, the trapped woman is spiritually carried back to the scene of her first communion, and begins to feel a spiritual contentment that transcends her physical situation. She does not dream of any deliverance here; "long ago stripped of any expectation, she was experiencing in her divine rapture how mystically true it is that 'he that dwelleth in the secret place of the Most High shall abide under the shadow of the Almighty'" (89).

Surely the religious tenor of the young wife's spiritual "deliverance" is in keeping with the didactic nature of the story's closing scene, but only momentarily are the themes and voice of the female community overshadowed by Christian rapture. Spofford's ironic juxtaposition of "witchcraft" and Christianity leads directly to the third and most pivotal point where the wife stops singing. In the throes of spiritual ecstasy, the young wife catches sight of her family below her:

> I do not know if it were the mother instinct that for a moment lowered her eyes,—those eyes so lately riveted on heaven, now suddenly seeing all life-long bliss possible. A thrill of joy pierced and shivered through her like a weapon, her voice trembled in its course . . . (90)

With the appearance of her family, the wife's hold on what should be more "important" priorities is shaken. Thus, the introduction of the husband and child at "Circumstance's" close does not merely supply a dramatic close to the wife's ordeal. Instead, her family's appearance works to *restore* the woman's momentarily lost identity as wife and mother. (Tellingly, the young woman is otherwise nameless throughout Spofford's tale.) With her reestablishment in the domestic community she has always known, the wife's momentary acceptance of death—along with its promise of Heavenly recompense—is forsaken. Thus, the woman's lost voice at such a key point in the narrative denotes not silence at all, but the desperate, muted cry of a wife and mother, which Spofford no doubt intended her female audience to "hear" perfectly. Spofford prepares her reader for what might otherwise seem an abrupt reversal in the woman's thinking by showing that the priorities of the domestic world are, in fact, never really eclipsed by her religious "awakening." For "Circumstance" to work, the wife's instantaneous abandonment of spiritual rapture for the hope of "all life-long bliss" must seem more immediate—more "real"—than might an outcome in keeping with a didactic Christian moral. By fostering a sense of "community" with her female audience, Spofford encourages an identification with her protagonist that remains viable not only throughout the wife's extraordinary ordeal but, more important, throughout the usurpation of Christian spirituality by woman-centered priorities. Although the reader soars with the wife to spiritual heights, the woman's wavering voice and thoughts of home are repeated reminders that she is "one of us," making her voice and story "real" despite such surreal circumstances.

In a somewhat similar fashion, the elder Elizabeth Stuart Phelps's "The Angel Over the Right Shoulder" (1852) overlays a story of women's community and women's voice with the gloss of Christian morality.[18] Mrs. James is unendingly dissatisfied with herself and her life because her hectic domestic schedule affords little time for anything else. "What would you think," she asks her husband, "if you could not get an uninterrupted half hour to yourself, from morning till night?" (156). Mr. James smugly asserts that all his wife lacks is a proper "system" (157), and proposes a one-month "experiment" in which Mrs. James abandon her roles as wife and mother for two hours each day and lock herself into her room with her books. Of course, the month passes quickly with nearly nothing accomplished; the unrelenting responsibilities of domestic care are forever summoning Mrs. James from her supposed "refuge." Disheartened but not surprised by the experiment's dismal outcome, Mrs. James looks on the upcoming New Year as a continuation of her empty existence:

> She thought of her disappointment and the failure of her plans. To her, not only the past month, but the whole past year seemed to have been one of fruitless effort—all broken and disjointed. . . . She had accomplished nothing that she could see, but to keep her house and family in order, and even this, to her saddened mind seemed to have been but indifferently done. (161)

Mrs. James falls asleep and dreams of a woman—a housekeeper—who is fastidiously watched by two angels, "the angel over the right shoulder" recording in his golden book even the smallest domestic duty the woman performs. Mrs. James recognizes the woman as her-

self, and she awakens to a "new existence" (164) and new appreciation of her life as wife and mother.

The message of "The Angel Over the Right Shoulder," as expressed in its closing New Year's Day "rebirth," seems remarkably
clear. The wife realizes that all the angel requires of her is "faithful-
ness and patience," and she readily adopts the submissive and satisfied attitude her dream inspires:

> Now she could see plainly enough that, though it was right and important
> for her to cultivate her own mind and heart, it was equally right and
> equally important to meet and perform faithfully all those little house-
> hold cares and duties on which the comfort and virtue of her family de-
> pended. . . . (164)

As in "Circumstance," however, the story's plot and seemingly unam-
biguous meaning frame somewhat less apparent women's issues that
work to undermine the story's "moral." Of course, the Christian
virtues of self-sacrificing service and cheerful submissiveness were
doubtless viable themes for many in Phelps's audience. Moreover, the
message of Christian duty might well be seen to have fairly "universal" appeal, with the closing didactic tone and message equally accessible to all Phelps's Christian readers. However, such a focus on
Phelps's closing moral is made problematic by the story that leads up
to the final message, for clearly much of "The Angel Over the Right
Shoulder" is not written for "everyone." Specifically, well over half of
Phelps's story is dominated by the domestic details of Mrs. James's
life, which undoubtedly reflected the lives of Phelps's female readers
in a way alien to a male audience. Indeed, throughout her tale,
Phelps paints a distinct picture, not merely of domestic responsibility but of the *frustration* that frequently accompanies such work. By
prefacing her Christian moral with Mrs. James's domestic drudgery,
Phelps sets up an essential tension between the reality presented in
the story's beginning and the dream that closes the tale. For, in the
end, Phelps's use of women's shared domestic existence serves to call
into question the meaningfulness and effectiveness of the very
"moral" the story presents.

The story opens with Mrs. James's exasperated exclamation,
"There! a woman's work is never done" (156) and proceeds to set
down in remarkable detail all the tedious tasks and daily "emergen-
cies" that flood the hours of this weary housekeeper. The entire

month of the proposed experiment is a patchwork of lost mittens, un-expected callers, loose buttons, crying children, and uncooperative servants, and each interruption to Mrs. James' "study time" works only to heighten her sense of dissatisfaction:

> She was conscious of yearnings for a more earnest life than this. Unsatis-fied longings for something which she had not attained often clouded what, otherwise, would have been a bright day to her. . . . (161–62)

Significantly, Phelps makes clear that Mrs. James's frustration is nei-ther shared nor understood by her husband. Mr. James's confidence that his wife "[has] no evils to endure" reveals more of his ignorance than his callousness, and Mrs. James accordingly replies, "That is just all you gentlemen know about it" (156). When Mr. James proposes the experiment that will supposedly grant his wife some free time, Mrs. James hesitates: "She felt almost sure that his plan would be quite impracticable, for what does a man know of a woman's work?" (157). Mr. James is so clueless regarding his wife's frustration that he truly cannot see his own complicity in it; after interrupting her study time to have a shirt mended, Mr. James tells his wife, "I am sure *I* did not hinder you long" (159). Mrs. James's frustration is decidedly spe-cific to her housekeeper role, and the details that Phelps supplies to convey the wife's dissatisfaction are surely ones that many of Phelps's female readers knew firsthand.

Because Phelps's representation of Mrs. James's unending duties is so "real," the wife's frustration becomes "real" as well for readers who themselves live a housewife's existence. Tellingly, the sight of her sleeping daughter sends Mrs. James into her sad meditation, and her subsequent dream is in part brought on by the wish "that she could shield that child from the disappointments and mistakes and self-re-proach from which the mother was then suffering" (162). In her dream, Mrs. James is a "looker-on" (163) who watches the dutiful housewife and the Angel's fastidious recording of the woman's good works. But this distance between herself and the woman in the dream is erased when Mrs. James recognizes herself as the beleaguered housewife. In similar fashion, the domestic details which *are* the first part of the story work to encourage an identification between Phelps's "real" housewife (Mrs. James) and the female reader. Mid-dle-class female readers *share* Mrs. James's frustration, extending the frustration into their own similar experiences, and this shared dissatisfaction renders the "compensation" of the story's moral tellingly ambiguous. Of course, "The Angel Over the Right Shoulder" supplies a "cure" for the wife's troubles, but the corrective can come only in the form of a dream (or the promised dream of an afterlife.) For Mrs. James and her female audience, the "real" remains essentially unchanged, and the shared women's language of domestic drudgery at times speaks much louder in Phelps's story than does the closing message of Christian duty.

Thus, "The Angel Over the Right Shoulder" engages its female audience through an ingenious subversion. In order to share in the story's Christian moral, the reader must first be drawn in by the story's representations of domestic drudgery. Like Mrs. James, the reader must recognize *herself* as the frustrated woman whose acts are forever scrutinized and judged. The very identification which must precede the promised Christian reward, however, works to undercut the real power of that reward. In the story, only the work and the frustration are "real"—the reward remains far off and dreamlike.

Women's domestic language, in fact, offers an alternative compensation for women, a "reward" embodied in the very sharing of women's language itself. The Christian moral of Phelps's tale is presented through the familiar device of God's angels watching over human endeavors and recording both good and evil in a "golden book" (163). But the good works that the woman in the dream performs are distinctly domestic in nature, reflecting a specifically female world:

> Sometimes, she did but bathe the weary feet of her little children, but the angel over the *right shoulder*—wrote it down. Sometimes, she did but patiently wait to lure back a distant truant who had turned his face away from the distant light, but the angel over the *right shoulder*—wrote it down. Sometimes, she did but soothe an angry feeling or raise a drooping eyelid, or kiss away a little grief; but the angel over the right shoulder—*wrote it down.* (163; emphasis Phelps's)

In her dream, Mrs. James realizes that everyday tasks are significant because they are being *written*—because someone else will subsequently read the record of the woman's life—and Mrs. James longs to reach out and give hope to the woman in the dream by telling her that "her life's work was all written down—every item of it" (164). Similarly, Phelps's story is the "golden book" that records the domestic language women share. The true cure the story offers for women's difficult lives is that their frustration is made real through

profound loneliness and her endeavor to reach out to the isolated woman.

Indeed, Jewett tells *this* story from the outset, her opening paragraph on Maine's seafaring heritage introducing the themes of crossing distances, making connections, and viewing experience within its larger—sometimes imperceptible—frame:

> the sea captains and the captains' wives of Maine knew something of the wide world, and never mistook their native parishes for the whole instead of a part thereof . . . (293)

The opening theme of crossing distances informs the scenes leading up to the visit, for the two women "put out across country as one puts out to sea" (300), with Mrs. Todd acting as "commander of the expedition" (306) which will travel the psychological bridge between Abby Martin and the Queen. In explaining her unique bond with Queen Victoria, Abby details the "birthright" (322) that connects their lives:

> We were born the same day, and at exactly the same hour, after you allow for all the difference in time. My father figured it out sea-fashion. Her Royal Majesty and I opened our eyes upon this world together; say what you may, 'tis a bond between us. (315)

Abby explains how she too married a man named Albert "and all by chance," and tells how she named her own children after those of her "mate" (316). Abby allows Mrs. Todd and the narrator to visit her best room where she displays her collection of pictures and newspaper clippings of the Queen, each trimmed in elaborate handmade framing. Ann Romines observes that Abby's "sisterhood" with Queen Victoria is expressed in markedly domestic language and asserts that housekeeping is the "birthright" that joins the two women:

> Abby has domesticated her image of the distant sister-queen, claiming Victoria's public life as a precious part of her privacy. Constructing frames for the queen's newspaper portraits, placing flowers at her shrine, and even assigning her a special teacup, she makes the queen her sister by including her in the language of her housekeeping.[22]

Indeed, Abby wistfully imagines that Victoria is "a beautiful housekeeper . . . as good a mother as she's been a queen" (317).

Nevertheless, defining Abby's "sisterhood" with Victoria exclusively through Abby's role and vision as housekeeper fails to address the true complexity of her identity as "The Queen's Twin," since it does not recognize the motives behind Abby's need to be this "sister." Moreover, such a focus ignores the overall structure of the story, in that it overlooks the visit scene's position within the larger tale of Mrs. Todd's relationship to Abby. Certainly many of the parallels that Abby draws between her own life and the Queen's have a domestic context, but Abby readily recognizes the vast differences between their lives as well: ". . . our stations in life are set very different. I don't require what the Queen does, but sometimes I've thought 't was left to me to do the plain things she don't have time for" (317). Similarly, Abby remarks that she never had a third daughter, as did the Queen, and tells how she often longed for a daughter to stay at home with her: "But if only one of us could have a little Beatrice, I'm glad 't was the Queen" (316). Abby does not simply use housekeeping to render her twin "identical" to herself; instead, Abby has developed a concept of *complementary* lives, creating for herself this grand "sister" who offers fulfillment through the knowledge that Abby's life is tied to another woman's.

Moreover, Abby believes that the Queen senses their special bond as well. Abby relates to the narrator and Mrs. Todd how she bore a hard voyage as ship's cook so that she could get a glimpse of Queen Victoria, and how upon arrival at London she literally ran to the palace:

> just as I worked to the front o' the crowd by the palace, the gates was flung open and out she came; all prancin' horses and shinin' gold, and in a beautiful carriage there she sat; 't was a moment o' heaven to me. I saw her plain, and she looked right at me so pleasant and happy, just as if she knew there was somethin' different between us from other folks. (320)

Abby, overcome with emotion recounting this "meeting," tells her listeners, "there hasn't been no friend I've felt so near to me ever since" (321). Abby's deep emotional need to have such a "sister" in her life is further evidenced in her increasing reliance on the Queen's "friendship" as her own life grows more solitary. Abby tells of walking alone in the woods and confiding in Victoria all her troubles and of the Queen's assuring her that "we must have patience" (322). She dreams of the two women, "young as ever we was," holding hands and walking together through fields, and wonders aloud, "I'd like to know if she ever has that dream too" (323). Abby's desire to bridge the vast spaces between herself and Queen Victoria is so intense that she one day pretends that Victoria is coming to pay a call and tells how she prepared a grand supper "sort of tellin' myself a story all the time" (324). Of course, the Queen does not arrive, but Abby's "story" of the longed-for visit inspires her to welcome a passing cousin whom she had always shunned in the past. Thus, Abby's imagined sharing with Queen Victoria leads to actual sharing within her more immediate community of women.

Similarly, the "story" of Abby's "sisterhood" works to create a sense of community between Abby and her female listeners. When Abby entrusts her guests with the story of the Queen's "visit," she states: "I never told this to a livin' soul before, but I feel you'll understand" (324). Certainly Abby's listeners *do* understand, and when Abby confesses it was "childish" of her to behave so, Mrs. Todd replies: "No, I guess you wa'n't the first one who's got supper that way, Abby" (325–26). In fact, Mrs. Todd herself picks up the threads of Abby's storytelling, commenting how much she would like to have Abby's royal "guest" make a trip to Green Island and pay a call on Mrs. Todd's mother.

By sharing her story of sisterhood with other women, Abby is able to enjoy a "real" sisterhood with her listeners, an understanding that lends dignity to what might otherwise be deemed a pathetic fantasy. The true purpose of Jewett's community story is created by the coming together of the visit scene and the scenes between Mrs. Todd and the narrator framing it. Early on in the story, Mrs. Todd confesses that she had long intended to call on Abby, but only upon her chance visit does she come to see her own complicity in her neighbor's lonely fantasy life:

> [Abby] was speaking o' some o' the facts to me today, an' you'd think she'd never done nothing but read history. I see how earnest she was about it as I never did before. (298)

Indeed, Mrs. Todd's half-spoken intent in telling the narrator about her visit with "The Queen's Twin" is to entice the other woman to pay a return visit to Abby's home. Thus, much like in "The Angel Over the Right Shoulder," Mrs. Todd fosters understanding and a sense of community among women by creating an *audience* for Abby Martin's storytelling. As Abby recalls the moment she and the Queen "met," the narrator and Mrs. Todd silently attend to the tale: "One could not say much—only listen" (321). And, of course, Mrs. Todd's parting remark that "it ain't as if we left her all alone" (328) underscores the visit's objective—to soothe Abby's loneliness and assuage Mrs. Todd's conscience. Without this women's-community context, the long-anticipated visit in Jewett's story is largely devoid of meaning, since the reader can only either mock Abby or pity her. But, by positioning the visit with Abby Martin not as a cause by as an *effect* of Abby's storytelling, Jewett creates the context of women's community that makes the scene meaningful.

Further, because Jewett's readers shared in the female "community" the Mrs. Todd story fosters, the reader doubtless was less inclined to view Abby's need for communion with some other woman as twisted or pitiful. Thus, just as Mrs. Todd's sense of women's community becomes the context for Abby's fantasy-tale, the *reader's* understanding of Mrs. Todd's motives and actions creates a community context for Jewett's tale. The visit to "The Queen's Twin" is not so much the climax of the story's action as it is a catalyst for the action which is women's community-building. "Community" in Jewett's story therefore *becomes* action, something women knowingly and deliberately *do*.

Another example of women's narratives creating community through "sisterhood" is Mary E. Wilkins Freeman's "Sister Liddy" (1891).[23] In Freeman's tale, the old women at the village poorhouse combat the indignity of destitution with daily "competitions" in which they compare and bicker over the relative splendor of their "past glories" (92). Old and crippled Polly Moss, however, is never a participant in such contests, since she had never owned anything that might compare to the other women's finery:

> Polly Moss alone had never spoken. She alone had never had anything in which to take pride. She had been always deformed and poor and friendless. . . . Everyday, when the others talked, she listened admiringly, and searched her memory for some little past treasure of her own, but she could not remember any. (92–93)

Polly finally decides to invent such a "treasure," and the inhabitants of the almshouse are shocked to hear her inject into their conversation, "You'd orter have seen my sister Liddy" (93). In the weeks that follow, Polly moves from outside the circle of women to the group's center, painting a lovely and fantastic picture of her much beloved sister:

> Every day Polly Moss was questioned and cross-examined concerning her sister Liddy. She rose to the occasion; she did not often contradict herself, and the glories of her sister were increased daily. Old Polly Moss, her little withered face gleaming with reckless enthusiasm, sang the praises of her sister Liddy as wildly and faithfully as any minnesinger his angel mistress, and the old women listened with ever-increasing bewilderment and awe. (96)

Although the poorhouse women "could not make up their minds whether to believe or disbelieve" (96), there is certainly little doubt in the reader's mind concerning Polly's fabrication, for Freeman's narrative outlines plainly the unlikelihood of such a relationship in Polly's life. Similarly, the story's closing "confessional" scene in which Polly states, "I never had any sister Liddy" (98), is anticlimactic in terms of revealing new or unexpected information; when Polly summons the other old women to her bedside, can there really be any reason but to reveal to them her deception? Freeman's earlier depiction of both the almshouse "contests" and Polly's alienation from the home's community of bickering women creates a scenario in which the reader anticipates fully the story's closing scene. In view of the fact that there is no real "suspense" here, how did "Sister Liddy" engage Freeman's reader? What function did Polly's deception serve, since it obviously was never intended to fool Freeman's audience? And what purpose might the very *predictability* of Freeman's closing scene have served in creating meaning?

Significantly, Polly's fictitious past glories are showered on an equally illusory *sister,* and not imagined for Polly herself. Of course, this aspect of her fiction is due, in part, to the physical deformity which would have made the other women even more suspicious of the story's veracity. But, more importantly, Polly's Sister Liddy is the child of Polly's friendlessness rather than her material poverty. Polly knows full well what a sister would mean to her audience of desperately lonely old women whose very circumstance speaks to the scarcity of such a fortunate and caring relative. As with Jewett's sister story, "Sister Liddy" relies on the reader's shared understanding of women's communities to explain the need for a "sister," since such crucial motives for Polly's deception remain largely unsaid. Like Abby's "twin" in "The Queen's Twin," Polly's invented sister connects her with the community of women by making Polly a *storyteller*. Polly obtains a place by gaining the voice long denied her: "Polly went on; she was not to be daunted; she had been silent all this time; and now her category poured forth, not piecemeal, but in a flood, upon her astonished hearers" (94). Indeed, Polly does not merely gain an opportunity to speak but "one-ups" the other speakers in a way they cannot rebuke; the almshouse women can compare and belittle each other's material wealth, but none can discount the emotional worth of a *sister*, especially one as fine as Liddy.

The prized nature of sisterhood underpins the real focus and impact of Freeman's closing confessional scene. Freeman's audience is never asked to believe Polly's sister story. The very falseness of Polly's tale, however, creates the scene's true pathos; not only has Polly been bereft of any physical comforts or material goods, but she has been largely cut off from women's compassion and connections her entire life. In asserting to the almshouse women that she too had once been loved and cared for, Polly claims her long-denied position as a *woman*, and not the "cretur" or "objeck" (84) that the others call her. Indeed, in Freeman's story, Polly comes "alive" only when she has her sister, her imagined relationship creating an opportunity to connect with others that had never before been available to her. Similarly, Polly's Sister Liddy works to make the old woman come "alive" for Freeman's reader. "Sister Liddy" works because of the female readers' shared understanding of why Polly creates her sister and how this sister transforms Polly in the eyes of other women. In "The Queen's Twin" and "Sister Liddy" the author uses sisterhood to tell the story of how otherwise isolated women reposition themselves to within a circle of women. The "miracle" of women creating community for themselves springs from the unsaid acknowledgment that even the most outcast woman may be someone's "sister."

Jewett's and Freeman's stories both detail one woman's relationship to a very specific female community. As Lillian Faderman observes, such individual ties were the foundation of a larger, more directly political "community" among nineteenth-century women:

> In nineteenth-century America close bonds between women were essential both as an outlet for the individual female's sensibilities and as a cru-

cial prop for women's work toward social and personal betterment in man's sullied and insensitive world.[24]

This new, expanding definition of "women's work" saw unprecedented numbers of middle-class women organize and take on a broad array of social and political causes, from the establishment of local orphanages and almshouses to the abolition of slavery. Of course such efforts were often part of much broader nineteenth-century movements to deal with the "dependent, defective, and delinquent classes" perceived to be expanding beyond control due to advancing industrialization and immigration.[25] Significantly, as Estelle Freedman notes in "Separatism as Strategy: Female Institution Building and American Feminism, 1870–1930," women's "formal" organizations for social and political reform were built primarily on existing female networks and notions of female "sisterhood." Referring specifically to the Women's Rights Movement, Freedman states:

> Although the women's movement of the late nineteenth century contributed to the transformation of women's social roles, it did not reject a separate, unique female identity. . . . Rather, [women] preferred to retain membership in a separate female sphere, one which they did not believe to be inferior to men's sphere and one in which women could be free to create their own forms of personal, social, and political relationships. The achievements of feminism at the turn of the century came less through gaining access to the male domains of politics and the professions than in the tangible forms of building separate female institutions.[26]

Further, Mary Ryan observes how many of the women's social organizations of the 1830s and 1840s "worked through informal personal associations, the sustained, everyday contacts between neighbors and kin, social networks which were especially familiar and comfortable to women."[27] Thus, nineteenth-century middle-class women's public/political "communities" largely took their shape through a re-envisioning of womanhood that defined women "by the extension, rather than the rejection, of the female sphere."[28]

Women's collective efforts in social reform also served as important avenues for expression, empowerment, and self-definition for many middle-class women. Religious and temperance crusades, calls for legislative reforms to grant women rights to property and their own children, societies to help widowed and destitute women, movements to form women's trade unions, all gave voice to issues and values that many women considered fundamental to their unique experience. The nineteenth-century women's "community" gave women's concerns a public forum and allowed middle-class women opportunities to enact large-scale change not possible through individual efforts. The relative effectiveness of women's "community" activities no doubt contributed to the solidarity that further took hold as women increasingly identified themselves through their group affiliation. For example, in studying the American Female Moral Reform Society, Smith-Rosenberg notes how the Society afforded women "a new consciousness of power," since its assertion of women's right to alter male behavior also allowed women to "forge a sense of their own identity."[29] Smith-Rosenberg observes how the Female Moral Reform Society "quite consciously sought to inspire in its members a sense of solidarity in a cause peculiar to their sex,"[30] and how the Society was specifically committed to "the creation of a feeling of sisterhood among all morally dedicated women."[31] Similarly, Lillian Faderman asserts that women's ties became stronger and even more important as women ventured into the male world of social and political action because women's reform activities "often were fueled by the sisterhood of kindred spirits who were righting a world men had wronged."[32]

Many nineteenth-century women's reform activities were aimed directly at improving the lives of other women, and not merely middle-class women. Although women's reform organizations often did have predominantly middle-class memberships, the "female institution building" that Freedman discusses frequently directed its efforts toward social ills that disproportionately affected women in general, if not specifically toward the needs of poor, working, and minority women. The efforts of middle-class women to bridge social distances between women through reform and charitable works was again born of their growing group-consciousness; increasingly, women were told that it was not merely unchristian but *unwomanly* to ignore the plight of their less-fortunate "sisters."

In *Woman in the Nineteenth Century* (1845), for instance, Margaret Fuller parallels American "ladies" to the women thieves and prostitutes in prison, demanding directly of her female audience, "Now I ask you, my sisters, if the women at the fashionable house be not answerable for those women being in the prison?" Fuller then urges her reader to seek out and help such degraded "sisters": ". . . [G]ive them tender sympathy, counsel, employment. Take the place of mothers, such as might have saved them originally."[33] Similarly, Sarah Grimke, in a letter of 1837, "On the Condition of Women in the United States," begins by discussing the faulty, sporadic education of fashionable ladies and housewives, but then goes on to decry the unfair wages allotted to working-class women. Grimke's attention turns next to "another class of women in this country, to whom I cannot refer without feelings of the deepest shame and sorrow"—namely, female slaves.[34] Grimke passionately details the physical and moral degradation of these "American women" and, like Fuller, specifically calls to task other women for their sisters' suffering:

> Can any American woman look at these scenes of shocking licentiousness and cruelty, and fold her hands in apathy, and say, "I have nothing to do with slavery"? *She cannot and be guiltless.* (emphasis, Grimke's)[35]

Of course, nineteenth-century women's reform movements did not go unscathed by the evils of class and racial bigotry, as was most readily demonstrated in the rift between abolitionist and non-abolitionist suffragists in the early women's movement. Remarks such as those by Fuller and Grimke, however, speak to the real sense of *duty* women were supposed to have for each other, a sentiment that informs many of the short stories dealing with women's reform issues.

For example, Lydia Maria Child uses the themes of women's sisterhood and common duty to each other to advance her abolitionist message in "The Quadroons" (1842) and "Slavery's Pleasant Homes" (1843) by exposing the unique plight of slave women: the licentiousness of white men in a system designed to allow masters full sexual liberty with their "property."[36] "Slavery's Pleasant Homes," in particular, presents white and black women's shared victimization under the slave system to incite indignation and sympathy in white female readers. Marion and her servant, Rosa, are raised as "foster sisters" (1809), enjoying a mutual love in spite of the social distinctions slavery has imposed. Shortly after Marion's marriage, however, the women's "sisterhood" is jeopardized by the lustful advances of Marion's husband, Frederic. Upon discovering Frederic's sexual encounter with Rosa, Marion is resentful and strikes her foster sister for the first time in her life. In Child's story, however, what the two women share again overcomes slavery's divisive influence, and Marion and Rosa turn to each other for support and understanding:

"Oh, mistress, I am not to blame. Indeed, indeed, I am very wretched."
Marion's fierce glance melted into tears. "Poor child," she said, "I ought
not to have struck you; but, oh Rose, I am wretched, too." The foster-sis-
ters embraced each other, and wept long and bitterly . . . (1810)

Jean Fagan Yellin has noted that plot and characters such as those in
"Slavery's Pleasant Homes" have become "mythic" in American antebellum literature, and that "like other mythologists, [Child] presents
types, concentrating on patterns of actions in her dramas of blacks
and whites, slaves and masters, men and women."[37] As Child's subti-
tle, "A Faithful Sketch," suggests, "Slavery's Pleasant Homes" is intended to showcase prototypical episodes representative of slavery's
pervasive evil. Nonetheless, to Child's nineteenth-century readers,
such figures and actions needed to appear "real" in order for the
story to achieve its intended goal; to "work," the abolitionist tale must
inspire identification, outrage, and then action. "Slavery's Pleasant
Homes'" effectiveness is achieved largely through women's relationships, specifically through the story's covert message of women's
shared destiny despite apparent differences in circumstance. Child
places her morality fable within the women's sphere, which most
white middle-class female readers would recognize immediately.

As the story's ironic title suggests, Child's focus is how slavery cor-
rupts the very heart of the women's sphere—the home. White and
black women are presented as "sisters," an emotional bond which
supposedly overshadows the social/economic relationship of mis-
tress-slave. Significantly, the fate of the story's two women is indelibly
joined because of their sisterhood, for both Marion and Rosa are
made "wretched" by Frederic's villainy not just to themselves but to
each other. By emphasizing the two women's *sameness,* despite their
seemingly contrasting positions, Child invites her female reader to
acknowledge and share in this "community" of oppressed, violated
women. Of course, Marion's and Rosa's misery play out quite differently in the story; disobeying Frederic's edict not to visit her own husband, Rosa is beaten to death while pregnant with what is most likely
her master's child. Still, Rosa's death further works to emphasize
women's particular victimization under slavery, for the brutal murder
of a young *mother* would surely strike many of Child's female readers
"close to home." In Child's story, slavery renders marriage a mockery
(for both white and black women), threatens to turn "sisters" into en-
emies and overthrows the values of the women's sphere as embodied

in the mother figure. As such, Child's short story is very much a precursor to Harriet Beecher Stowe's impassioned appeal to women in *Uncle Tom's Cabin* (1852):

> And you, mothers of America,—you, who have learned, by the cradles of your own children, to love and feel for all mankind. . . . I beseech you, pity those mothers that are constantly made childless by the American slave trade! And say, mothers of America, is this a thing to be defended, sympathized with, passed over in silence?[38]

Child's story is an example of how white middle-class women's growing sense of "community" in nineteenth-century America was manifested in efforts to reach out to less fortunate "sisters," both in society and in fiction. It is also important here to consider how African-American women's own sense of "community" is relevant to their short stories. A more careful consideration of the ways nineteenth-century black women's particular experience structured short fiction casts new light on some African-American tales that have been broadly labeled "didactic" in nature. For example, Frances E. W. Harper's "The Two Offers" (1859)—the first short story published by an African-American woman—is typically seen as a cautionary tale denouncing the evil influence of alcohol and calling on women to cultivate fully their mental and moral beings.[39] Fearful of becoming an old maid, young Laura Lagrange accepts what seems the better marriage proposal, only to suffer "the bitter agony that is compressed in the mournful words, a drunkard's wife" (1977). Laura soon dies an abandoned, broken woman, but her "old maid" cousin, Janette, learns from Laura's mistake and uses Laura's example to motivate her own life of self-reliance and good works.

Frances Smith Foster has noted that the story's "generic" descriptions of physical features have led some critics to assume that the characters are white. Foster contends, however, that "given its author and its publisher [the *Anglo-African Magazine*], this is a mistaken assumption."[40] But Foster's comments themselves assume the "evidence" of the characters' racial identity lies primarily outside the story in Harper's and the periodical's racial affiliation, and that the story, in and of itself, is somehow "aracial." Such a view reflects the belief that the influence of the black female experience is manifested primarily in complexion (the characters', the authors', or the readers'). Deeming "The Two Offers" "aracial" denies Harper's participation in the black women's community and overlooks the influence of that community in shaping the story. In discussing interpretive strategies for approaching Harper, Paul Lauter notes the necessity of seeing Harper in her cultural context: "Any institutional arrangement which systematically separates the texts from the world in which they are embedded arrests our capacity to read them."[41] How might nineteenth-century African-American women writers' sense of their black "sisterhood" have structured Harper's story?

A 1903 story by Ruth D. Todd offers revealing insights into reading not just "The Two Offers" but other African-American women's community tales. In many respects, "The Folly of Mildred: A Race Story With a Moral," echoes Harper's much earlier tale, but here the context of the black female community and its role in women's "uplift" is more overt.[42] The story opens with two young middle-class black women debating whether the beautiful but haughty Mildred James should be invited to join their club in which "morals, social reform, literature, elocution and later-day etiquette are to be studied deeply, and discussed thoroughly" (241). Although Mildred has been the subject of "whispered comments" (240), Laura argues that the young woman's apparent moral laxity is the very reason why Mildred should be encouraged to join their circle:

> She must be made to understand that her tastes and manners are forced and exaggerated, her mind decidedly uncultivated, and her morals in sad need of repair. It is not to be wondered at that the "colored" American girl is regarded by the Anglo-Saxon as utterly devoid of all morality when such girls as Miss James . . . display such shameful conduct and set such disgraceful examples. (240–41)

Black women's sense of themselves in community motivates Laura's interest in Mildred, and she explains to her friend that it is their "duty" to "reform . . . straying sisters" (241).

"The Folly of Mildred" deals with African-American women's experience in defining Mildred's "folly" as well. Her own complexion "exceedingly light" (242), Mildred has become a vain, uncaring, superficial woman expressly because she deems other darker women in her community "far beneath her" (243). Mildred declines Laura's offer and focuses her attention instead on two somewhat different offers. Robert Thompson is handsome and loving, but he is "too dark" (245) and too poor for Mildred to accept his proposal. Lemuel Flemings, however, is "very light" and "was reputed to have lots of money" (246). Like the poor heroine in Harper's story, Mildred soon learns the full repercussions of her shallowness. Her husband a hopeless gambler, Mildred becomes "a veritable slave" in her drudgery, while Laura (who has married Mildred's cast-off lover) ends happily "in a whirl of fashionable society" (249).

The women's community issues that shape "The Folly of Mildred" clearly place Todd's story within a black female context. The call to combat negative stereotypes concerning black women's virtue, the need for black women to help fallen "sisters," the bitter irony of color discrimination among blacks, the dire consequences for black women of social vices were concerns that many African-American women readers surely understood well, as the countless articles written by black women addressing such concerns exemplify. It is therefore interesting to consider the extent to which a black female audience "read" the community story in Harper's tale as well and to examine the ways in which "The Two Offers" spoke to African-American women. The undeniable parallels between Todd's "race story" and Harper's "aracial" story demonstrates that "The Two Offers" was likely read by African-American women as a black women's community story, and that African-American women never mistook Harper's characters as either white or "generic."

Laura Lagrande's outcome is revealed early in Harper's tale, with the narrator "fast-forwarding" to the deathbed scene, then using flashbacks to fill in the details of Laura's ill-fated marriage. The real uncertainty, then, is *Janette's* fate in the story, since, from the outset, Janette is cast in sharp contrast to her foolish and unfortunate cousin. Too self-reliant to accept others' charity, Janette works feverishly to make her life "not a thing of ease and indulgence, but of conquest, victory, and accomplishment" (1,974). After witnessing Laura's pathetic ending, Janette "turned from that death-bed a sadder and wiser woman" (1,979) and considers her life "a high and holy mission" (1,980) to help others.

Here, the message of one's moral duty to her community is clear and much in keeping with Harper's "uplift" agenda. Perhaps less obvious, Harper relies on her readers' sense of women's community to shape her message, for the story suggests that Janette's choice proves better not just for herself but for everyone around her. In Harper's story, women's choices have larger, *community* implications, and Harper's narrator expounds on what should be the "true aim of female education," namely the development of "perfect woman-hood":

> Is it any wonder, then, that so many life-barks go down, paving the ocean of time with precious hearts and wasted hopes? that so many float around us, shattered and dismasted wrecks? that so many are stranded on the shoals of existence, mournful beacons and solemn warnings for the thoughtless . . . ? (1,976)

Harper's title thus alludes to the "two offers" facing women such as Janette: a shallow life focused on only women's "affectional nature" with men, or the "true woman's" life of works within her community (1,976). As a black women's community story, "The Two Offers" works through the story's unstated assertion that what happens to Laura is relevant to the reader because black women's lives and destinies are interrelated. Asserting the "aracial" status of Harper's story positions a nineteenth-century white female reader as an "insider" who hears and understands fully the "unsaid" meanings in the story. However, a revisioning of "The Two Offers" as an African-American women's community story renders this assumption invalid.

The nineteenth-century sentiment that women were all part of the larger community of women inspired writers to use their fiction to address the concerns of "other" women as well. Writers such as Child, Stowe, and Fanny Fern often wrote on middle-class women's duty to poor and working women, calling on the reader's sense of community with these different women to advance their causes. Stowe's "The Seamstress" (1843) taps into the fears of its middle-class female audience by presenting a middle-class woman reduced to poverty upon her husband's death. Mrs. Ames and her daughters must resort to sewing to earn their meager living, and Stowe chronicles the women's constant labors through hunger and illness. Stowe's "story," however, lies not in such sad details but in the relationship between these working women and the middle-class housekeepers for whom they toil. In "The Seamstress," the struggling family's difficulties are exacerbated by the uncaring, unthinking women who demand too much, pay too little, and take not even the slightest interest in the women they employ. Stowe's message of women's duty to the working poor is demonstrated in her repeated use of the word *duty* in describing the customers' unthinking treatment of working women. One housekeeper "*felt it a duty*" as an economist to pay the lowest price possible for the sewing, but "she did not consider that, by paying liberally those who were honestly and independently struggling for themselves," she was really performing a significant act of charity.[43] "The Seamstress" closes by making explicit the story's community-consciousness intent:

> We have given these sketches, drawn from real life, because we think there is in general too little consideration on the part of those who give employment to those in situations like the widow here described.[44]

Although Stowe's story is expressly written to underscore privileged women's obligation to their working sisters, Stowe, all the while, assumes that her reader, in fact, already holds this belief; if the reader did not beforehand share some sense of "community" with such women, Stowe's "real life" sketches would have failed not merely to inspire change but even to *be* the reform story that Stowe had intended.

In a similar fashion, Fanny Fern, in "The Working Girls of New York" (1868), writes not to create but to awaken middle-class women's consciousness regarding their ties to working women. Fern touches on middle-class readers' indifference by noting: "While yet your breakfast is progressing, and your toilet unmade" the "working-girls" are already trudging off to the factory.[45] Fern emphasizes her readers' ties to the "girls" by describing the grinding toil of employment in a hoop-skirt factory:

> If you are a woman you have worn plenty; but you little thought what passed in the heads of these girls as their busy fingers glazed the wire, or prepared the spools for covering them, or secured the tapes which held them in their place. *You* could not stay five minutes in that room . . . .[46]

By addressing her reader and inviting that reader to envision herself in the working girl's shoes, Fern renders these "other" women less alien and shows middle-class women's real responsibility to their working "sisters." In this sense, Fern's sketch is much more directly a statement of readers' duty to working wretches than is, for example, Herman Melville's dreamlike allegory of working women, "The Paradise of Bachelors and the Tartarus of Maids" (1855).[47] It is interesting that such overtly didactic works as those by Child, Stowe, and Fern were generally dismissed by twentieth-century critics and, in part, fell into obscurity because of their social reform messages; clearly, when viewed in a women's community context, the stories' true artistic power lies precisely in their ability to motivate readers through the readers' ties to "other" women.

The ability of middle-class women to "reach out" to other women through their stories is necessarily limited, and the nature of such limitations again reflects the assumption of common experience inherent in nineteenth-century "sisterhood." Women's shared communication and unsaid understanding are important structural devices in many women's community stories, but what women share as women cannot always overcome other social differences. The inability and inappropriateness of middle-class women speaking to and for *all* women is addressed in "A Mistaken Charity" (1887), in which Mary E. Wilkins Freeman pokes light fun at middle-class women's confidence that they know what is best for other women. Mrs. Simonds is a kind woman "bent on doing good," but "she always did it in her own way."[48] When Mrs. Simonds and her charitable associates decide that Harriet and Charlotte Shattuck would be more comfortable in the "Old Ladies Home" than at their dilapidated shack, the "benevolent" women never truly understand the impoverished sisters' need for privacy, dignity, and self-determination. Harriet and Charlotte tolerate the "charity" for two months and then, in a truly comic scene, the two ancient women "run away," leaving the Home's attendants scrambling to find them. The "mistake" in the well-meaning women's "charity" lies in the assumption that Harriet and Charlotte would gladly trade their independence for the more middle-class accommodations provided by the Home. In presenting a story in which middle-class women's priorities are not those of all women, Freeman demonstrates a critical self-awareness seldom shared by her middle-class contemporaries. Auerbach maintains that the women's community can readily "create itself," but the prerequisite commonality of experience behind this "miracle" is at times not attainable, even in the world of separate spheres. In "A Church Mouse," Hetty is able to win the crowd because, in essence, she is speaking to "a jury of her peers." But when the jury/audience is markedly different, the encoded meanings in women's community stories may not be heard.

The limitations of middle-class women's stories in "reaching out" to working-class women may perhaps be best observed by examining some short fiction by nineteenth-century working women and considering the ways working-class stories used the work experience to create meaning. Nineteenth-century working women's fiction presents special difficulties for scholars, since it is seldom clear to what extent middle-class publishers influenced, edited, or "improved" working women's stories. With advancing industrialization and the rise in number of women entering the industrial workforce, late-nineteenth-century debates concerning the working woman's occupation, family situation, and morality became more prominent and heated in middle-class America. Consequently, as Laura Hapke observes in *Tales of the Working Girl,* the working-class woman quickly emerged as a popular character in American mass-market fiction which adapted familiar melodramatic plots to accommodate the new working-class ingenue:

> Infusing the formulaic subgenre with a quasi-sociology of the female work place, the working girl's literary imaginers soon included the genteel practitioners of the Lower East Side seduction tale, who catered to middle-class preferences for the eleventh-hour rescue and the romanticized poor. . . . Whether their orientation was sentimental or social Darwinist, romantic or naturalisitic, such writers produced a body of work that explained the embattled urban working girl to an audience with no relation to her other that a condescending one.[49]

Hapke writes that mainstream "working girl" fiction—"produced largely by and for middle-class consumption"—voiced middle-class America's disapproval of women's paid work as a disruption of and threat to the separate spheres paradigm.[50]

As the social-reform fiction of writers such as Fern and Stowe demonstrates, not all middle-class fiction presented the working girl in a negative or condescending light. But, as the historian Nancy Woloch has noted, the separate spheres ideology of the middle-class had little bearing on urban working women's real world.[51] How, then, did working women's visions of the "working girl" differ from the popular literary representations of her? Nineteenth-century middle-class women's stories at times sought to "reach out" to less fortunate "sisters." Did working-class women's stories express this cross-class "sisterhood" as well? And how might such stories speak to a "sisterhood" unique to working women? While acknowledging the at times insurmountable difficulty in distinguishing working-class women's texts from middle-class editors' appropriations, examining the ways that working women's realities fashioned the unsaid in women's community stories illuminates not only the stories themselves but also middle-class women's relationship to the stories.

A germane example of nineteenth-century working-women's literature, *The Lowell Offering* is a product of what Benita Eisler calls the "Mill Girl Subculture" of New England mill workers in mid-nineteenth-century America.[52] In studying the correspondence of mid-century mill women, Thomas Dublin notes that the factory experience dramatically shaped the lives of mill women in such fundamental areas as the ages they married, the spouses they chose, the number of children they bore, and the places they settled. As Dublin states, "The mill experience, even when it lasted only a few years, had a permanent impact on women."[53] As discussed briefly in chapter 3, *The Lowell Offering* entertained a dual audience: while the *Offering* courted the attention and approval of middle-class "outsiders," the works published were written by factory girls expressly for their working sisters. How might the Lowell "subculture"—with its associated connotations of a closed, distinct community—have structured the "mill girl" community stories that appeared in these first printed writings "by and about American blue-collar women"?[54]

Seen as a women's community story, "The Patchwork Quilt" (1845) voices the importance of women's ties and traditions as represented in women's art forms.[55] The "old maid" in the story sees her quilt as "a bound volume of hieroglyphics" (150), and invites her female audience to share in her "reading" of the quilt: "I must tell you, and then you will not wonder that I have chosen for this entertainment my *patchwork quilt*" (150). The narrator then relates that the quilt symbolizes her life within the community of women, for each piece of carefully worked cloth reestablishes for the old woman the long-gone female ties that have shaped her world. Calico from her own childhood gowns, dress pieces from her mother, sister, and friends, each quilt patch is a short story within the full narrative of a life, and the lonely woman describes with great feeling the quilting party where many hands worked to fashion her treasured heirloom. As in middle-class women's stories such as Freeman's "Sister Liddy" and Jewett's "The Queen's Twin," the need of isolated women to create a women's community for themselves was the key to deciphering the story's "hieroglyphics" for the middle-class reader; "The Patchwork Quilt" relies on the "invisible" thread of women's ties to piece together the story's overall meaning for such women readers.

The patchwork quilt, however, does not simply tie the old woman to a female community, since it links her directly to the *working* world as well. The quilt is now valued by the woman because it represents her past relationships; when it was being constructed, however, the quilt symbolized future hopes for economic advancement. In reminiscing about the quilt's origins, the narrator tells how her labor taught her more than sewing skills:

> How much, too, I learned of the world's generosity in rewarding the efforts of the industrious and enterprising. How many pieces in that quilt were presented because I "could sew," and *did sew,* and was such an adept in sewing. . . . What predictions that I could some day earn my living by my needle—predictions, alas! that have most signally failed. (151)

Recalling her feelings "of exaltation, of self-dependence, of *self-reliance*" (153) in earning her first money from work, the narrator now confesses,

> To do for myself—to earn my own living—to meet my daily expenses by my own daily toil, is now a task quite deprived of its novelty, and Time has robbed it of some of its pleasure. (153)

Significantly, the quilt's "hieroglyphics" equally voice the realities of the narrator's life as a woman and a *worker;* the story speaks to a certain pride and dignity in women's paid work not often found in middle-class stories in which the necessity of paid work commonly represents an unanticipated drop in social/economic position. Of course, economic "self-reliance" (an ironic allusion to Emerson?) has proven unattainable for this working woman, since she is telling her life story from her "old-maid's hall" (150). Yet the realities of a lifetime of labor and an unenviable fate as an impoverished spinster surely make poignant a working-class woman's reading of both the quilt and the story. In this working-class community story, then, women's relationships and women's work are inextricable, for the patchwork quilt itself is created only when women come together and work. "Work" thus defines the community within the "mill girl subculture" in a way fundamentally different from the housework that informs the sphere of nineteenth-century middle-class women.

In similar fashion, the 1841 *Lowell Offering* story, "Susan Miller," uses women's community issues to appeal to its dual audience.[56] After the death of Susan's drunkard father, the farm girl dutifully sets out to work off the family's debt by getting a job at Lowell. As with other *Lowell Offering* stories, "Susan Miller" caters to middle-class readers through its rather opaque effort to dispel pervasive biases against mill girls and foster a sense of commonality between the reader and the "girls." In a lengthy scene between Susan and Deacon Rand, the story addresses nearly all mid-century objections to working girls, with Susan deftly countering each charge against mill life and factory girls. And, of course, middle-class concerns over the working girls' impact on separate spheres and family life are quieted in the story's assertion that paid work was a temporary endeavor for most mill operatives:

> Every morning the bells pealed forth the same clangor, and every night brought the same feeling of fatigue. But Susan felt, as all factory girls feel, that she could bear it for a while. There are few who look upon factory labor as a pursuit for life. It is but a temporary vocation; and most of the girls resolve to quit the Mill when some favorite design is accomplished. (181)

By assuring middle-class readers that these working women are not really much different from themselves, "Susan Miller" asserts common values and objectives among women that outweigh overt class differences. Significantly, the short story emphasizes the "strong friendships" (181) Susan forms among the factory girls, touching on the theme of female companionship which echoes throughout middle-class women's short fiction. Such female ties are contrasted to the indifference Susan's supposed beau shows upon her departure for Lowell and the painful disappointment Susan feels when she learns later of his marriage. Much like the "jilted" women in many nineteenth-century middle-class women's tales, Susan has female friends who prove true; years after she leaves the mill, she "always thinks of Lowell with pleasure" (182). Thus, "Susan Miller's" heroine is cast firmly not just in middle-class morality but in middle-class perception of the women's sphere, rendering Susan a fitting vehicle to dispel class prejudices and misconceptions.

Middle-class women's reading of the story notwithstanding, "Susan Miller" was surely a working-class story to the mill operatives who also read it, since the realities of work and the "mill girl subculture" unmistakably shape the tale. From the outset, there is really no question for working-class readers what Susan will do upon her father's death, not just because of where the story appears but because so many mill operatives had experienced similar circumstances prior to joining Lowell. For the working woman, then, the lengthy exchange between Susan and Deacon Rand on mill girl life functions much differently than it does for middle-class "outsiders." The working woman is not reading to see if Susan does the right thing but to reconfirm her belief that she herself has done so. Further, just as Susan's plan of action is more or less set for the working-class reader from the opening, so too is the story's conclusion. Susan pays off her family's debt and remains at Lowell a year more to secure her future comfort when she returns home for good. The certainty of Susan's success is achieved largely through the *universality* of Susan's experience which *The Lowell Offering*'s mill-girl readers could hardly miss; from the long stage ride from home, to the shared room at the boarding house, to the deafening whir of the spindles, the "story" in "Susan Miller" is the challenge of newness that every Lowell girl had known to some degree. "Susan Miller" relies on the working-class reader's understanding of Susan's ordeal to make the fairly predictable ending "work," since surely such a reader herself had to hold at least some faith in her own triumphant departure from Lowell. By incorporating into the tale the mill girl's sense of herself as part of the singular world of factory women, "Susan Miller" provides the desired ending for the reader's *own* story still in progress. The reassuring predictability of the story's outcome (which detractors could point to as propaganda aimed at the middle class), in fact, underlies the tale's appeal for the working woman.

In some respects, *The Lowell Offering* presents a special case in working-women's literature, since the *Offering* enjoyed national—indeed, international—fame for displaying (as the *Offering*'s editors often proclaimed) the "mind among the spindles." Yet *The Lowell Offering* was not without its detractors, as was most keenly demonstrated in the blistering public debate between Sarah G. Bagley and the magazine's editor, Harriet Farley, over allegations that the *Offering* failed to show the true hardships of mill life. In the *Voice of Industry* for July 17, 1845, Bagley blasted the *Offering*:

It is, and always has been under the fostering care of the Lowell Corporations, as a literary repository for the mental gems of those operatives who have ability, time and inclination to write—and the tendency of it ever has been to varnish over the evils, wrongs, and privations of a factory life. This is *undeniable*, and we wish to have the *Offering* stand upon its own bottom,

instead of going out as the united voice of the Lowell Operatives, while it
wears the Corporation lock and their apologizers hold the keys. . . .[57]

That *The Lowell Offering* was the product of a select group of operatives who, as Bagley states, had the "ability, time and inclination to
write" does not, in and of itself, position the *Offering* outside the
broader mill-girl subculture, since many of the magazine's contribu-
tors actively shared in the factory experiences of their less articulate
sisters. Moreover, it is important to note that *The Lowell Offering* was
criticized as unrepresentative of mill-girl subculture primarily with regard to its political message and not in relation to the literary language and style of the stories. If, as Bagley and others charged, *The
Lowell Offering* was the propagandistic tool of management to gloss
over worker discontent, "Susan Miller" demonstrates how women's
relationships and the nineteenth-century conception of women's
"community" played a key role in such agendas, as well as suggesting
how working-class women writers and readers may have had quite different agendas of their own.

As such working women's fiction reveals, socially prescribed def-
initions of women's "communities" comprise the "unsaid" text in
nineteenth-century women's community stories. While some writers'
class or racial assumptions may inadvertently, if you will, limit a story's
effectiveness or appeal, in other instances nineteenth-century middle-class attitudes appear more *deliberately* exclusionary, more keenly
aware of the "community's" boundaries. For instance, Charlotte
Perkins Gilman's "The Yellow Wallpaper" (1892) has been widely
read by feminist critics as the quintessential expression of nineteenth-century women's "entrapment" as symbolized by the "creeping woman" behind the wallpaper's "bars."[58] Elizabeth Ammons for
one has noted the themes of women's solidarity and shared destiny
in Gilman's text:

It is not . . . simply a story about the desire for escape from male control.
It is also a story about the desire to escape *to* a female world, a desire to
unite with the mother, indeed with all women creeping and struggling in
growing numbers, through the paper, behind the wall.[59]

However, in an insightful study of racial and class issues in Gilman's
works, Susan S. Lanser calls to task the assumption that the "The Yellow Wallpaper" speaks to *all* women and asserts that the time has

come "to stop reading a privileged, white, New England woman's text as simply—a woman's text."[60] Focusing not on the infamous patterns of the story's wallpaper but instead on the paper's long-overlooked *yellowness*, Lanser convincingly demonstrates how prevalent nineteenth-century racial prejudices against "yellowness" (as it applied "not only to the Chinese, Japanese, and light-skinned African-Americans but also to Jews, Poles, Hungarians, Italians, and even the Irish")[61] are encoded into the young wife's abhorrence of the "repellent . . . revolting . . . smouldering unclean yellow" wallpaper.[62] Similarly, in a study of Gilman's political radicalism, Mary A. Hill notes how Gilman (like many of her nationalist associates) expressed frequently a "condescending paternalism" toward those she deemed culturally or racially inferior.[63] By locating "The Yellow Wallpaper" within the "psychic geography" of middle-class Anglo-American at the turn of the century,[64] Lanser reveals the inherent deceptiveness of "The Yellow Wallpaper's" status as a "universal" women's text, since surely "yellow" women experienced a much different relationship to the paper's "hideous . . . unreliable . . . infuriating" color than did white readers.[65] The "female world" Ammons and others cite as the story's refuge for "creeping" women is an exclusively white middle-class female world, in which "other" struggling women are not invited to join.

Gilman similarly demonstrates the uniquely middle-class nature of the "community" in some women's stories in the 1911 short story "Old Mrs. Crosley." The children grown and the house efficiently run by a handful of well-selected servants, Mrs. Crosley feels useless and isolated, and she wonders bitterly, "Of what earthly use am I?"[66] Confiding her troubles to her clergyman, Mrs. Crosley learns from him that she possesses "a rare and invaluable talent": "There are thousands of women who can cook and sew and clean to one who can manage servants."[67] The minister then chides Mrs. Crosley for not using her talent "for the good of the community," and explains that, in fact, it is her "plain duty" to do so: "If you don't do it . . . it will be no longer due to ignorance, but to selfishness and cowardice." In Gilman's story, it seems that Mrs. Crosley has been commissioned by God to run "a really intelligent intelligence office," but plainly the community to whom she owes this charge is exclusively middle-class.[68] Quite tellingly, in *Women and Economics* (1898), Gilman lamented how the undeniable differences between middle-class women and their servants threatened "domestic privacy,"[69] and she

expounded on the servant woman's position as "outsider" in a middle-class home:

> [She is] a complete stranger, a stranger not only by reason of new ac-
> quaintance and of the false view inevitable to new eyes let in upon our se-
> crets, but a stranger by birth, almost always an alien in race, and, more
> hopeless still, a stranger by breeding, one who can never truly under-
> stand.[70]

To "alien" working women (largely comprising the "yellow" women
Lanser describes), "Old Mrs. Crosley" has little appeal; indeed, Mrs.
Crosley's sisterly "duty" lies primarily in helping other middle-class
women best to exploit this "resource."

"The Yellow Wallpaper" and "Old Mrs. Crosley" are examples of
women's community stories that foster "community" through *exclusion* by using, in these instances, white middle-class experience as the
criteria for sharing in the writer-reader "sisterhood" of short story encoding. Even stories that ostensibly aim to "reach out" to other
women evidence similar cultural prejudices. For example, Stowe's
story on women's duty to the working poor, "The Seamstress," seeks
to impress upon middle-class readers their responsibility to help the
"deserving" poor, clearly making a distinction between "decent" and
"self-respecting" poor women and some "other" sort of needy
women.[71] Such stories reveal how the assumed understanding between short story writer and reader often extends to tacitly understood biases as well.

The ways that encoded meanings can be used to unite some
women while excluding others is well illustrated in Catharine Maria
Sedgwick's "Fanny McDermot" (1845) in which the poor, innocent
heroine is seduced by a wealthy, sophisticated "gentleman."[72] After
living briefly as a kept woman and bearing a child, the abandoned
Fanny is unable to find work because of her marred reputation. Weak
and friendless, Fanny hopelessly roams the streets where she and her
child catch fever; Fanny later dies at "The Tombs," pathetically
clutching to her breast her dead infant. Ostensibly, Sedgwick's story
is presented as a warning to unwary young women, an invitation to
see themselves in Fanny's position and to recognize that the wretched
girl's troubles might well be their own:

> It is not to draw tears, which flow too easily from susceptible young read-
> ers, that the following circumstances are related, but to set forth dangers

to which many are exposed, and vices which steep the life God has given as a blessing, in dishonour, misery, and remorse. (113)

However the women's community issues in Sedgwick's story are not limited to readers' identification with the heroine, since "Fanny McDermot" also speaks to women's direct ties to "fallen women." In particular, the story exposes respectable women's complicity in the "double standard" that banishes poor Fanny from decent society while excusing the actions of her seducer. Despite Fanny's abilities as seamstress, Mrs. Emly denies Fanny a position explaining that "No respectable lady would take a person of that kind into her house" (138). Yet, Mrs. Emly not only tolerates Fanny's seducer, Mr. Sydney, in her home but hopes to make a match between him and her daughter, Augusta. When Fanny tells Mrs. Emly that Sydney was her seducer, Mrs. Emly does not fault Sydney but merely reasons that "pretty girls in [Fanny's] station are apt to go astray" (149). Augusta repudiates her mother's illogical distinction between Fanny and Sydney stating, "I see no difference, excepting that the one is the strong party, the other the weak,—the one the betrayer, the other the betrayed" (141). By implicating readers in Fanny's suffering, Sedgwick attacks middle-class women's scorn for lower-class girls "gone astray" and highlights women's hypocritical role in maintaining the "double standard." Paralleling such women to the spiteful mob in the gospel, the narrator contends, "Bold, and hardened indeed, must have been the human creature who could have cast the first stone at [Fanny]" (130).

In denouncing "hardened" women's treatment of each other, "Fanny McDermot" calls on women not merely to pity but to help fallen women, to follow Margaret Fuller's advice of the same year and give degraded women "tender sympathy, counsel, employment."[73] Fanny's situation becomes "fatal" not when Sydney deserts her, but when *other women* do through their punctilious refusal to allow Fanny any respectable means of self-support. Augusta Emly condemns her mother's "irrational and unchristian" treatment of Fanny, and then asks, "As women, as professed followers of Christ, my dear mother, ought we not to help her out of the pit into which she has fallen?" (141). Again women are pressed to acknowledge their duty "as women" to their unfortunate sisters, and when Fanny is cast out, Augusta remarks, "May God be more merciful to her than we have been" (140).

Mutual responsibility, shared sexual destiny, "womanly" compassion—all function to awaken women's sense of community in Sedgwick's tale. Also at work in "Fanny McDermot," however, are more subtle mechanisms of tapping into middle-class women's consciousness, devices that rely on the audience's shared racial prejudices. "Fanny McDermot" fosters "sisterhood" between respectable middle-class ladies and fallen women, but this "community" is created at the expense of Irish women. At the beginning of the story, Fanny's Aunt Sara Hyat voices the common bigotry against her Irish neighbors, forbidding her niece to associate with "them Irish cattle" and lamenting the Lord's apparent will "that they should overrun us like frogs and locusts" (116). Of course, Fanny counters that her Irish neighbors are in fact "very kind" (116) and, at least overtly, this is the attitude assumed by the story's narrator as well. Indeed, the Irish women in the story repeatedly come to Fanny's aid, taking her in without harsh judgment and seeing her as the victim that the story's community-building message stresses. A closer look at Sedgwick's Irishwomen, however, uncovers standard negative stereotypes. For example, Fanny's friend Mrs. O'Roorke has a "drunken husband" (143), although Mrs. O'Roorke herself has given up whiskey, "thank God and Father Matthew" (134). Most significantly with regard to the story's plot, the Irish families in "Fanny McDermot" are unspeakably filthy, seemingly upholding Aunt Sara's sentiment the "you can scarce call them human creturs" (116). The story's narrator contrasts the apartments of Fanny and her Irish neighbors, the latter's home most characterized by "a superfluidity of dirt":

> On entering Mrs. Hyat's rooms, you are in another country, the tenants are obviously Americans, it is so orderly, quiet, and cleanly, and rather anti-social. (114)

Likewise, Fanny is extremely grateful when Mrs. O'Roorke offers to take her in, but simply cannot stay with the well-meaning Irishwoman because the home is so dirty:

> Fanny looked round upon the "bit place," and it must be confessed that she sickened at the thought of living in it, even with the sunny kindness of its inmates, or of leaving her little snowdrop of a baby there. The windows were dim with dirt, the floor was unwashen—a heap of kindlings were in one corner, potatoes in another, and coals under a bed, none the tidiest. Broken victuals on broken earthen plates stood on the table, and all contrasted too strongly with the glossy neatness of her aunt's apartment. Surely Fanny was not fastidious. (143)

The closing emphasis on the "rightness" of Fanny's revulsion is telling. The focus on Irish squalor is used to render Irishwomen the "other," to segregate them and their homes from "American" women's lives and ways. (Note as well the racial undertones to the disparity between the Irish and Fanny's "snowdrop" baby.) Surely the "unsaid" appeal to middle-class readers in Sedgwick's "community" story is the encoded admonition that these filthy "foreign" women are behaving in a more Christian, more American, more *womanly* fashion than are Fanny's "real" sisters. The unsaid community message in Sedgwick's handling of the Irish is that such Irishwomen are a poor substitute for middle-class women's compassion and solidarity. In "Fanny McDermot" the "unformulated miracle" of the women's community "creating itself" proves, at least in part, to be merely a racist sleight-of-hand. Clearly, Sedgwick's tale implies a somewhat selective nature to women's shared experience and "sisterhood."

The socially defined construct of the women's community in Sedgwick's story lends important insights into why many nineteenth-century women's community stories fell into obscurity. As advances in the women's movement allowed more and more women access to hitherto closed fields, the world of "separate spheres" (and its resulting commonality of experience) began to decline. Estelle Freedman discusses the effect of the rapidly emerging "new woman" on women's shared perceptions:

> The self-consciously female community began to disintegrate in the 1920s just as "new women" were attempting to assimilate into male-dominated institutions. At work, in social life, and in politics . . . middle-class women hoped to become equals by adopting men's values and integrating into their institutions. A younger generation of women learned to smoke, drink, and value heterosexual relationships over female friendships in their personal lives. At the same time, women's political activity epitomized the process of rejecting women's culture in favor of men's promises of equality.[74]

To many such "new women" the domestic culture and values of women only a generation earlier were just as "foreign" as were the lives of Sedgwick's "alien" Irishwomen to a middle-class audience. As women increasingly sought to assimilate into the male world, the assumption that a female audience would automatically "read" the unsaid nuances of the women's community could not so readily be made. Instead of speaking to a homogeneous middle-class female

community, twentieth-century women writers were faced with the
new challenge of being an "out" group within the male literary tradition. The appeal of many nineteenth-century women's community
tales rests largely on their ability to bridge women's lives through a
recognition of shared experience; when such works could no longer
bring women together, they really ceased being "community stories"
for many twentieth-century women.

Nineteenth-century middle-class women's stories provide a
unique opportunity to look into a closed, "secret" female world where
women's ties offered a sort of refuge for otherwise oppressed pas-
sions, energies, and ambitions. In reading women's relationship stories as encoded statements of women's need for each other, readers
today also are allowed a glimpse of what these stories might have
meant to the women who wrote and first read them. In this sense, the
lost world of "separate spheres" is emotionally revived, since our
growing understanding breathes new life into both women's stories
and the community such stories detail. Perhaps in our increasing appreciation of nineteenth-century women's relationship stories lies
the real "unformulated miracle" Nina Auerbach describes; by studying the power of women's relationship stories, readers today come to
see how individual hands linked to form the closed circle of nineteenth-century middle-class experience. Virginia Woolf once said,

> a woman's writing is always feminine; it cannot help being feminine; at its
> best it is most feminine: the only difficulty lies in defining what we mean
> by feminine.[75]

What Woolf saw as the real "difficulty" in assessing women's writing
provides the true key for unlocking nineteenth-century women's relationship stories. The myriad of ways that nineteenth-century writers defined their womanhood points to the many avenues for exploring women's experience, but each path is merely one strand in
the complex network of relationships mapping the "feminine" world.
At one point in Glaspell's "A Jury of Her Peers" Mrs. Hale states,

> We live close together, and we live far apart. We all go through the same
> things—it's all just a different kind of the same thing! (279)

In its capacity to voice simultaneously women's differences and sameness, "feminine" writing is, indeed, "at its best."

Notes

CHAPTER 1: "BOLD, FRANK, AND TRUTHFUL": "GREAT BOOKS," ENCODED MEANINGS AND NINETEENTH-CENTURY WOMEN'S SHORT STORIES

Fanny Fern quote taken from (Sara Willis Parton), "The Working Girls of New York," *The Heath Anthology of American Literature*, 2d ed., vol. 1, gen. ed. Paul Lauter (Lexington, Mass.: D.C. Heath and Company, 1990), 1955.

1. Glaspell, "A Jury of Her Peers," *The Best Short Stories of 1917 and the Yearbook of the American Short Story*, ed. Edward J. O'Brien (Boston: Small, Mayourd and Company, 1918): 256–82. Hereafter cited parenthetically.

2. Pattee, *The Development of the American Short Story: An Historical Survey* (New York: Bilbo and Pannen, 1966), 152.

3. Ibid., 328.

4. Davidson, *Revolution and the Word: The Rise of the Novel in America* (New York: Oxford University Press, 1986), 45.

5. Woloch, *Women and the American Experience* (New York: Knopf, 1984), 132.

6. Voss, *The American Short Story: A Critical Survey* (Norman: University of Oklahoma Press, 1973).

7. Baym, "Melodramas of Beset Manhood: How Theories of American Fiction Exclude Women Authors," *American Quarterly* 33:2 (1981): 124.

8. McClave, "Introduction," *Women Writers of the Short Story: A Collection of Critical Essays* (Englewood Cliffs: Prentice-Hall, 1980), 4–5.

9. Davidson, 5.

10. Susan K. Harris, "'But Is It Any Good?': Evaluating Nineteenth-Century American Women's Fiction," *American Literature* 63.3 (1991), 52.

11. Kolodny, "A Map for Rereading: Or, Gender and the Interpretation of Literary Texts," *New Literary History* 11:3 (1980): 452.

12. Harris, "Evaluating," 44.

13. See Matthews, "The Philosophy of the Short-Story" ; Mary Rohrberger, "The Short Story: A Proposed Definition," 81; H. E. Bates, "The Modern Short Story: Retrospect," 74—all in *Short Story Theories*, ed. Charles E. May (Athens: Ohio University Press, 1976).

14. Hanson, "Introduction," *Re-reading the Short Story*, ed. Clare Hanson (London: Macmillan Press, 1989), 2.

15. Edgar Allan Poe, "Review of Twice-Told Tales by Nathaniel Hawthorne," *Great Short Works of Edgar Allan Poe*, ed. G. R. Thompson (New York: Harper & Row, 1970), 521.

16. Ibid., 520.

17. Ibid., 522.

18. Ibid., 521.

19. McClave, "Introduction," 2.

20. Iser, "Interaction Between Text and Reader," *The Reader in the Text: Essays on Audience and Interpretation,* ed. Susan R. Suleiman and Inge Crosman (Princeton: Princeton University Press, 1980), 109.

21. Ibid., 110–11.

22. Hanson, "'Things Out of Words': Towards a Poetics of Short Fiction," *Re-reading the Short Story,* ed. Clare Hanson (London: Macmillan Press, 1989), 25.

23. Fish, *Is There a Text in This Class? The Authority of Interpretive Communities* (Cambridge: Harvard University Press, 1980), 172.

24. Ibid., 171.

25. Schweickart, "Reading Ourselves: Toward a Feminist Theory of Reading," *Speaking of Gender,* ed. Elaine Showalter (New York: Routledge, 1989), 34.

26. Kolodny, "Dancing Through the Minefield: Some Observations on the Theory, Practice and Politics of a Feminist Literary Criticism," *Feminist Studies* 6:1 (1980): 10.

27. Ibid., 12.

28. Kolodny, "Map for Rereading," 463.

29. Ibid.

30. Baym, 124.

31. Gullason, "What Makes a 'Great' Short Story Great?" *Studies in Short Fiction* 26:3 (1989): 271.

32. Ibid., 269.

33. Ibid., 276.

34. Finke, *Feminist Theory, Women's Writing* (Ithaca: Cornell University Press, 1992), 172.

35. Gullason, 271.

36. Ibid., 269.

37. Schweickart, "Reading Ourselves," 34.

38. Miller, *Toward a New Psychology of Women* (Boston: Beacon Press, 1976), 10.

39. Thompson, "Introduction," *Great Short Works of Edgar Allan Poe,* ed. G. R. Thompson (New York: Harper & Row, 1970), 20.

40. Edgar Allan Poe, "The Cask of Amontillado," *Great Short Works of Edgar Allan Poe,* ed. G. R. Thompson (New York: Harper & Row, 1970), 496.

41. Finke, *Feminist Theory,* 154.

42. See Cott, *The Bonds of Womanhood: "Woman's Sphere" in New England, 1780–1835* (New Haven: Yale University Press, 1977), and "Passionlessness: An Interpretation of Victorian Sexual Ideology, 1790–1850," *Signs* 4 (1978): 219–36; also, Smith-Rosenberg, *Disorderly Conduct: Visions of Gender in Victorian America* (New York: Knopf, 1985); and "The Female World of Love and Ritual: Relations Between Women in Nineteenth-Century America," *Signs* 1 (1975): 1–29.

43. Kolodny, "Map for Rereading," 460; Gilbert and Gubar, *The Madwoman in the Attic: The Woman Writer and the Nineteenth-Century Literary Imagination* (New Haven: Yale University Press, 1979).

44. Schweickardt, "Reading Ourselves," 29.

45. Zagarell, "Narrative of Community: The Identification of a Genre," *Signs* 13 (1988): 504–505.

46. Linda K. Kerber, "Woman's Place: The Rhetoric of Women's History," *Journal of American History* 75:1 (1981): 28.

47. Evans, *Born for Liberty: A History of Women in America* (New York: Free Press, 1989), 86.

48. See Fox-Genovese, *Within the Plantation Household: Black and White Women of the Old South* (Chapel Hill: University of North Carolina Press, 1988); and Clinton, *The Plantation Mistress: Woman's World in the Old South* (New York: Pantheon Books, 1982).

49. Smith-Rosenberg, "Female World of Love and Ritual," 1–2.

50. Dobson, "The American Renaissance Reenvisioned," *The (Other) American Traditions: Nineteenth-Century Women Writers*, ed. Joyce W. Warren (New Brunswick, N.J.: Rutgers University Press, 1993), 170.

51. Faderman, "Lesbian Magazine Fiction in the Early Twentieth Century," *American Women Short Story Writers: A Collection of Critical Essays*, ed. Julie Brown (New York: Garland Publishing, 1995), 100.

52. Ibid., 102.

53. Dobson, "American Renaissance," 170.

54. Rich, "When We Dead Awaken: Writing as Re-Vision," *College English* 34:1 (1972): 18.

CHAPTER 2: "FAMILY SECRETS":
THE MOTHER-DAUGHTER RELATIONSHIP IN
WOMEN'S SHORT STORIES

Lucy Howard quote cited in Nancy M. Theriot, *The Biosocial Construction of Femininity: Mothers and Daughters in Nineteenth-Century America* (New York: Greenwood Press, 1988), 77.

1. Cited in Linda W. Rosenzweig, *The Anchor of My Life: Middle-Class American Mothers and Daughters, 1880–1920* (New York: New York University Press, 1993), 24.

2. Smith-Rosenberg, *Disorderly Conduct: Visions of Gender in Victorian America* (New York: Knopf, 1985), 32.

3. Cited in Rosenzweig, *Anchor of My Life*, 25.

4. See Ryan *The Empire of the Mother: American Writing About Domesticity, 1830–1860*, in the series *Women and History*, numbers 2/3, ed. Eleanor S. Reimer (New York: Haworth Press, 1982); Rosenzweig, *The Anchor of My Life: Middle-Class American Mothers and Daughters, 1880–1920* (New York: New York University Press, 1993); Lewis, "Mother's Love: The Construction of an Emotion in Nineteenth-Century America," *Social History and Issues in Human Consciousness: Some Interdisciplinary Connections*, ed. Andrew E. Barnes and Peter N. Stearns (New York: New York University Press, 1989): 209–29; and Dally, *Inventing Motherhood: The Consequences of an Ideal* (London: Burnett Books, 1982).

5. Smith-Rosenberg, "Female World of Love and Ritual," 16.

6. Theriot, *Bisocial Construction*, 76.

7. Lewis, "Mother's Love," 214.

8. Ibid., 224.

9. Hammer, *Daughters and Mothers: Mothers and Daughters* (New York: New York Times Book Company, 1975), xiii.

10. Susan Koppelman, "Introduction," *Between Mothers and Daughters: Stories Across a Generation*, ed. Susan Koppelman (Old Westbury, N.Y.: The Feminist Press, 1985), xv–xxxix.

11. Freeman, "On the Walpole Road," *American Women Regionalists 1850–1910*, ed. Judith Fetterley and Marjorie Pryse (New York: W.W. Norton, 1992), 306–14; hereafter cited parenthetically.

12. Poe, "The Philosophy of Composition," *Great Short Works of Edgar Allan Poe,* ed. G. R. Thompson (New York: Harper & Row, 1970), 528.

13. Koppelman, "Introduction," xxvi.

14. Reichardt, *A Web of Relationship: Women in the Short Stories of Mary Wilkins Freeman* (Jackson: University Press of Mississippi, 1992), 45.

15. Cited in Rosenzweig, *Anchor of My Life,* 25.

16. Koppelman, "Introduction," xx.

17. Ibid.

18. Ibid., xv.

19. Hammer, *Daughters and Mothers,* xiv.

20. Ibid., 17.

21. Zitkala-Sa, "The Trial Path," *American Women Regionalists, 1850–1910,* ed. Judith Fetterley and Marjorie Pryse (New York: W.W. Norton, 1992), 559–63; hereafter cited parenthetically.

22. Theriot, *Bisocial Construction,* 31.

23. Ibid., 33.

24. Chodorow, *The Reproduction of Mothering: Psychoanalysis and the Sociology of Gender* (Berkeley: University of California Press, 1978), 109.

25. Theriot, *Bisocial Construction,* 12.

26. Wharton, "The Quicksand," *The Collected Short Stories of Edith Wharton,* ed. R. W. B. Lewis (New York: Charles Scribner's Sons, 1968), 397–410; hereafter cited parenthetically.

27. Anderson, "The Untold Lie," *Winesburg, Ohio* (New York: Penguin Books, 1976), 202–209.

28. Hurst, "Oats for the Woman," *Between Mothers and Daughters: Stories Across a Generation,* ed. Susan Koppelman (Old Westbury, N.Y.: The Feminist Press, 1985): 82–112.

29. Smith-Rosenberg, "Beauty, The Beast and the Militant Woman: A Case Study in Sex Roles and Social Stress in Jacksonian America," *American Quarterly* 23 (1971): 583.

30. Theriot, *Bisocial Construction,* 25.

31. Freeman, "The Revolt of 'Mother'," *The Heath Anthology of American Literature,* vol. 2, gen. ed. Paul Lauter (Lexington, Mass.: D.C. Heath, 1990), 148–59; hereafter cited parenthetically.

32. Reichardt, *Web of Relationship,* 48.

33. Theriot, *Bisocial Construction,* 84.

34. Freeman, "An Autobiography," *Critical Essays on Mary Wilkins Freeman,* ed. Shirley Marchalonis (Boston: G.K. Hall, 1991), 66.

35. Ibid., 65.

36. Ryan, *The Empire of the Mother,* 149.

37. Freeman, "Old Woman Magoun," *The Heath Anthology of American Literature,* vol. 2, gen. ed. Paul Lauter (Lexington, Mass.: D.C. Heath, 1990), 159; hereafter cited parenthetically.

38. Cited in Mary A. Hill, *Charlotte Perkins Gilman: The Making of a Radical Feminist 1860–1896.* Philadelphia: Temple University Press, 1989, 196.

39. Bowen, "A Marriage of Persuasion," *Between Mothers and Daughters: Stories Across a Generation,* ed. Susan Koppelman (Old Westbury, N.Y.: The Feminist Press, 1985), 13–22; hereafter cited parenthetically.

40. Koppelman, "Introduction," xviii.

41. Phelps, "Old Mother Goose," *Between Mothers and Daughters: Stories Across a Generation,* ed. Susan Koppelman (Old Westbury, N.Y.: The Feminist Press, 1985), 23–41; hereafter cited parenthetically.

42. Koppelman, "Introduction," xxix.

43. King, "One of Us," *American Women Regionalists, 1850–1910*, ed. Judith Fetterley and Marjorie Pryse (New York: W.W. Norton, 1992), 380–81; hereafter cited parenthetically.

44. Williams, "After Many Days: A Christmas Story," *The Unforgetting Heart: An Anthology of Short Stories by African American Women (1859–1993)*, ed. Asha Kanwar (San Francisco: Aunt Lute Books, 1993), 39–52; hereafter cited parenthetically.

45. Washington, "Introduction," *Invented Lives: Narratives of Black Women 1860–1960* (New York: Anchor Press, 1987), xxi.

46. Bruck, "Black American Short Fiction in the Twentieth Century: Problems of Audience, and the Evolution of Artisitc Stances and Themes," *The Black American Short Story in the Twentieth Century: A Collection of Critical Essays*, ed. Peter Bruck (Amsterdam: B.R. Gruner, 1977), 2.

47. For discussions of the "tragic mulatta" as both a social construction and a literary device, see Christian, *Black Women Novelists: The Development of a Tradition, 1892–1976* (Westport, Conn.: Greenwood Press, 1980); Clinton, *The Plantation Mistress: Woman's World in the Old South* (New York: Pantheon Books, 1982); Hazel V. Carby, *Reconstructing Womanhood: The Emergence of the Afro-American Woman Novelist* (New York: Pantheon Books, 1982); Fox-Genovese, *Within the Plantation Household;* Jules Zanger, "The 'Tragic Octoroon' in Pre-Civil War Fiction," *American Quarterly* 18 (1966): 63–70; Catherine Juanita Starke, *Black Portraiture in American Fiction: Stock Characters, Archetypes, and Individuals* (New York: Basic Books, 1971).

48. Ries, "Mammy: A Story," *The Unforgetting Heart: An Anthology of Short Stories by African American Women (1859–1993)*, ed. Asha Kanwar (San Francisco: Aunt Lute Books, 1993), 81–83; hereafter cited parenthetically.

49. Theriot, *Bisocial Construction*, 31.

50. Brown, *"The Way of Peace," Between Mothers and Daughters: Stories Across a Generation*, ed. Susan Koppelman (Old Westbury, N.Y.: The Feminist Press, 1985): 45–60; hereafter cited parenthetically.

51. Koppelman, "Introduction," xx.

52. Jewett, "The Foreigner," *The World of Dunnet Landing. A Sarah Orne Jewett Collection*, ed. David Bonnell Green (Lincoln: University of Nebraska Press, 1962), 250–91; hereafter cited parenthetically.

53. Fetterley and Pryse, "Introduction," *American Women Regionalists, 1850–1910*, ed. Judith Fetterley and Marjorie Pryse (New York: W.W. Norton, 1992), 186.

54. Gardiner, "On Female Identity and Writing by Women," in *Writing and Sexual Difference*, ed. Elizabeth Abel (Chicago: University of Chicago Press, 1982), 188.

55. Chodorow, *Reproduction of Mothering*, 200.

56. Sigmund Freud, "Female Sexuality," *Sigmund Freud, Collected Papers*, vol. 5, ed. James Strachey (London: Hogarth Press, 1956), 254.

CHAPTER 3: "IN THE PRIVACY OF OUR OWN SOCIETY": WRITING FEMALE FRIENDSHIP AS STORY

Virginia Woolf quote taken from *A Room of One's Own* (New York: Harcourt Brace Jovanovich, 1929), 85–86.

Excerpt of letter taken from Smith-Rosenberg, "Female World of Love and Ritual," 2.

1. (Sarah) Margaret Fuller, *Woman in the Nineteenth Century: The Essential Margaret Fuller*, ed. Jeffrey Steele (New Brunswick, N.J.: Rutgers University Press, 1992), 347.

2. Ibid., 282.

3. Fuller, "(On Anna Barker), Journal, October 1842," *The Essential Margaret Fuller*, ed. Jeffrey Steele (New Brunswick, N.J.: Rutgers University Press, 1992), 22–23.

4. Ibid., 23.

5. Fuller, *Summer on the Lakes: The Essential Margaret Fuller*, ed. Jeffrey Steele (New Brunswick, N.J.: Rutgers University Press, 1992): 69–225; hereafter cited parenthetically.

6. Steele, "Introduction," *Essential Margaret Fuller*, ed. Steele (New Brunswick, N.J.: Rutgers University Press, 1992), xxiii.

7. Fuller, *Woman in the Nineteenth Century*, 347.

8. Fuller, "On Anna Barker," 23.

9. Smith-Rosenberg, "Female World of Love and Ritual," 9.

10. Ibid., 9–10.

11. Ibid., 24.

12. Ibid., 8.

13. Sahli, "Smashing: Women's Relationships Before the Fall," *Chrysalis* 8 (1979): 22.

14. Ibid., 18.

15. Martin, "Knights-Errant and Gothic Seducers: The Representation of Male Friendship in Mid-Nineteenth-Century America," *Hidden from History: Reclaiming the Gay and Lesbian Past*, ed. Martin Bauml Duberman, Martha Vicinus, and George Chauncey, Jr. (New York: NAL Books, 1989), 180.

16. Ibid., 174.

17. Ibid., 180.

18. Faderman, *Surpassing the Love of Men: Romantic Friendship and Love Between Women from the Renaissance to the Present* (New York: William Morrow, 1981), 152.

19. Ibid., 153.

20. Sahli, "Smashing," 21.

21. Smith-Rosenberg, "Female World of Love and Ritual," 14.

22. Ibid., 24.

23. Ibid., 28.

24. Bernikow, *Among Women* (New York: Harmony Books, 1980), 5.

25. Faderman, *Surpassing the Love of Men*, 162.

26. Koppelman, "Afterword," *Women's Friendships: A Collection of Short Stories*, ed. Susan Koppelman (Norman: University of Oklahoma Press, 1991), 291.

27. Cosslett, *Woman to Woman: Female Friendhsip in Victorian Fiction* (Brighton, Sussex: Harvest Press, 1988), 11.

28. Phelps, "At Bay," *Women's Friendships: A Collection of Short Stories*, ed. Susan Koppelman (Norman: University of Oklahoma Press, 1991), 19–37; hereafter cited parenthetically.

29. Bernikow, *Among Women*, 114.

30. Koppelman, "Afterword," 296.

31. Kessler, "Preface to 'At Bay'," *Women's Friendships: A Collection of Short Stories*, ed. Susan Koppelman (Norman: University of Oklahoma Press, 1991), 16.

32. Cary, "Charlotte Ryan," *Clovernook Sketches and Other Stories*, ed. Judith Fetterley (New Brunswick, N.J.: Rutgers University Press, 1987), 105–37; hereafter cited parenthetically.

33. "Ann and Myself: No Fiction," *The Lowell Offering: Writings by New England Mill*

Women (1840–1845), ed. Benita Eisler (Philadelphia: J.B. Lippincott, 1977), 192–96; hereafter cited parenthetically.

34. *Letters of Sarah Orne Jewett,* ed. Annie Fields (Boston: Houghton Mifflin, 1911), 126.

35. Jewett, "Miss Tempy's Watchers," *Women's Friendships: A Collection of Short Stories,* ed. Susan Koppelman (Norman: University of Oklahoma Press, 1991), 40–50; hereafter cited parenthetically.

36. Brown, "Joint Owners in Spain," in *Women's Friendships: A Collection of Short Stories,* ed. Susan Koppelman (Norman: University of Oklahoma Press, 1991), 53–67; Child, "The Neighbour-in-Law," in *Women's Friendships: A Collection of Short Stories,* ed. Susan Koppelman (Norman: University of Oklahoma Press, 1991), 6–15; both texts hereafter cited parenthetically.

37. Koppelman, "Afterword," 286.

38. Karcher, "Preface to 'The Neighbour-in-Law'," *Women's Friendships: A Collection of Short Stories,* ed. Susan Koppelman (Norman: University of Oklahoma Press, 1991), 5.

39. Faderman, *Surpassing the Love of Men,* 157.

40. Smith-Rosenberg, "Female World of Love and Ritual," 14.

41. Cott, *Bonds of Womanhood,* 187.

42. Faderman, *Surpassing the Love of Men,* 167.

43. Wharton, "Friends," *Women's Friendships: A Collection of Short Stories,* ed. Susan Koppelman (Norman: University of Oklahoma Press, 1991), 72–91; hereafter cited parenthetically.

44. Hackleman, "Preface to 'Friends'," *Women's Friendships: A Collection of Short Stories,* ed. Susan Koppelman (Norman: University of Oklahoma Press, 1991), 72.

45. Ibid.

46. Freeman, "Friend of My Heart," *The Uncollected Stories of Mary Wilkins Freeman,* ed. Mary R. Reichardt (Jackson: University Press of Mississippi, 1992), 197–211.

47. Howells, *The Rise of Silas Lapham* (New York: Signet Classics, 1963), 222.

48. Jewett, "Martha's Lady," *Atlantic Monthly* (October 1897): 523–33; hereafter cited parenthetically.

49. *Letters of Sarah Orne Jewett,* 112–13.

50. Hobbs, "Pure and Passionate: Female Friendship in Sarah Orne Jewett's 'Martha's Lady'," *Critical Essays on Sarah Orne Jewett,* ed. Gwen L. Nagel (Boston: G.K. Hall, 1984), 103.

51. *Letters of Sarah Orne Jewett,* 113.

52. Woolf, *A Room of One's Own,* 86.

53. Ibid., 88.

54. Faderman, *Surpassing the Love of Men,* 176–77.

55. Ruth Ashmore, "The Intense Friendships of Girls," *Ladies Home Journal* 6 (July 1898): 20.

56. Chopin, "The Falling in Love of Fedora," *American Women Writers: Diverse Voices in Prose Since 1845,* ed. Eileen Barrett and Mary Cullinan (New York: St. Martin's Press, 1992), 145–47.

57. *Letters of Sarah Orne Jewett,* 246.

58. Smith-Rosenberg, "Female World of Love and Ritual," 1.

59. Chodorow, *Reproduction of Mothering,* 199.

60. Ibid., 200.

61. Eichenbaum and Orbach, *Between Women: Love, Envy, and Competition in Women's Friendships* (New York: Viking, 1988), 20–21.

62. Janice G. Raymond, *A Passion for Friends: Toward a Philosophy of Female Affection* (Boston: Beacon Press, 1986), 3.

CHAPTER 4: PICKING UP "OTHER WOMEN'S DESTINIES": NINETEENTH-CENTURY WOMEN'S COMMUNITY STORIES

King quote is taken from "The Balcony," *American Women Regionalists, 1850–1910,* ed. Judith Fetterley and Morjorie Pryse (New York: W.W. Norton, 1995), 380.

Grimke quote is from *Letters on the Equality of the Sexes and the Condition of Woman, Letters on the Equality of the Sexes and Other Essays,* ed. Elizabeth Ann Barlett (New Haven: Yale University Press, 1988), 103.

1. Auerbach, *Communities of Women: An Idea in Fiction* (Cambridge, Mass.: Harvard University Press, 1978), 11.

2. See Smith-Rosenberg, *Disorderly Conduct: Visions of Gender in Victorian America* (New York: Knopf, 1985); and Welter, *Dimity Convictions: The American Woman in the Nineteenth Century* (Athens: Ohio University Press, 1976).

3. Cott, *Bonds of Womanhood,* 189.

4. Zagarell, "Narrative of Community," 499–500.

5. Ibid., 499.

6. Ibid., 507.

7. Ibid., 516.

8. Freeman, "A Church Mouse," *A New England Nun and Other Stories* (New York: Harper and Brothers, 1891), 407–26; hereafter cited parenthetically.

9. Romines, *The Home Plot: Women, Writing and Domestic Ritual* (Amherst: University of Massachusetts Press, 1992), 104.

10. Romines, *Home Plot,* 106–107; Lauter, "Teaching Nineteenth-Century Women Writers," *The (Other) American Traditions: Nineteenth-Century Women Writers,* ed. Joyce W. Warren (New Brunswick, N.J.: Rutgers University Press, 1993), 285.

11. Smith-Rosenberg, "Female World of Love and Ritual," 11.

12. Cott, *Bonds of Womanhood,* 190.

13. Ibid., 194.

14. Levy, *Fiction of the Home Place: Jewett, Cather, Glasgow, Welty, and Naylor* (Jackson: University of Mississippi Press, 1978), 229.

15. Romines, *Home Plot,* 17.

16. Spofford, "Circumstance," *The Heath Anthology of American Literature,* vol. 2, gen. ed. Paul Lauter (Lexington, Mass.: D.C. Heath, 1990), 83–92; hereafter cited parenthetically.

17. Shinn, "Preface to 'Circumstance'," *The Heath Anthology of American Literature,* vol. 2, gen. ed. Paul Lauter (Lexington, Mass.: D.C. Heath, 1990), 82.

18. Phelps, "The Angel Over the Right Shoulder," *Rediscoveries: American Short Stories by Women, 1832–1916,* ed. Barbara H. Solomon (New York: Penguin Books, 1994), 156–64; hereafter cited parenthetically.

19. Cott, "Passionlessness," 233–34.

20. Zagarell, "Narrative of Community," 500.

21. Jewett, "The Queen's Twin," *The World of Dunnet Landing. A Sarah Orne Jewett Collection,* ed. David Bonnell Green (Lincoln: University of Nebraska Press, 1962), 292–328; hereafter cited parenthetically.

22. Romines, *Home Plot,* 78.

23. Freeman, "Sister Liddy," *A New England Nun and Other Stories* (New York: Harper and Brothers, 1891), 81–98; hereafter cited parenthetically.

24. Faderman, *Surpassing the Love of Men,* 160.

25. James Leiby, *A History of Social Welfare and Social Work in the United States* (New York: Columbia University Press, 1978), 1.

26. Freedman, "Separatism as Strategy: Female Institution Building and American Feminism, 1870–1930," *Feminist Studies* 5 (1979): 514.

27. Ryan, "The Power of Women's Networks: A Case Study of Female Moral Reform in Antebellum America," *Feminist Studies* 5 (1979): 69.

28. Freedman, "Separatism," 518.

29. Smith-Rosenberg, "Beauty, the Beast and the Militant Woman," 578.

30. Ibid., 577.

31. Ibid., 576.

32. Faderman, *Surpassing the Love of Men*, 160.

33. Fuller, *Woman in the Nineteenth Century*, 329.

34. Grimke, *Letters on the Equality of the Sexes*, 59.

35. Ibid., 61.

36. Child, "The Quadroons," *Rediscoveries: American Short Stories by Women, 1832–1916*, ed. Barbara H. Solomon (New York: Penguin Books, 1994), 88–98; "Slavery's Pleasant Homes—A Faithful Sketch," *The Heath Anthology of American Literature*, vol. 1, gen. ed. Paul Lauter (Lexington, Mass.: D.C. Heath, 1990), 1,809–12; hereafter cited parenthetically.

37. Yellin, "Lydia Maria Child, 1802–1880," *Heath Anthology of American Literature*, vol. 1, gen. ed. Paul Lauter (Lexington, Mass.: D.C. Heath, 1990), 1,827.

38. Harriet Beecher Stowe, *Uncle Tom's Cabin* (New York: New American Library, 1981), 471–72.

39. Harper, "The Two Offers," *Heath Anthology of American Literature*, vol. 1, 2d ed., gen. ed. Paul Lauter (Lexington, Mass.: D.C. Heath, 1994), 1,973–80; hereafter cited parenthetically.

40. Foster, *Written By Herself: Literary Production by African American Women, 1746–1892* (Bloomington: Indiana University Press, 1993), 196.

41. Lauter, "Is Frances Ellen Watkins Harper Good Enough to Teach?" *Legacy* 5 (1988): 32.

42. Todd, "The Folly of Mildred: A Race Story with a Moral," *Short Fiction by Black Women, 1900–1920*, ed. Elizabeth Ammons (New York: Oxford University Press, 1991), 239–49; hereafter cited parenthetically.

43. Stowe, "The Seamstress," *Rediscoveries: American Short Stories by Women, 1832–1916*, ed. Barbara H. Solomon (New York: Penguin Books, 1994), 107.

44. Ibid., 110.

45. Fern, "Working Girls," 1,955.

46. Ibid., 1,956.

47. Herman Melville, "The Paradise of Bachelors and the Tartarus of Maids," *Great Short Works of Herman Melville*, ed. Warner Berthoff (New York: Harper & Row, 1969), 202–22.

48. Freeman, "A Mistaken Charity," *Rediscoveries: American Short Stories by Women, 1832–1916*, ed. Barbara H. Solomon (New York: Penguin Books, 1994), 369.

49. Hapke, *Tales of the Working Girl: Wage-Earning Women in American Literature, 1890–1925* (New York: Twayne Publishers, 1992), 3–4.

50. Ibid., 6.

51. Woloch, *Women and the American Experience* (New York: Knopf, 1984).

52. Eisler, "Introduction," *The Lowell Offering: Writings by New England Mill Women (1840–1845)*, ed. Benita Eisler (Philadelphia: J.B. Lippincott, 1977), 9.

53. Dublin, ed., *Farm to Factory: Women' Letters, 1830–1860*, 2d ed. (New York: Columbia University Press, 1993), 33.

54. Eisler, "Introduction," 41.

55. "The Patchwork Quilt," *The Lowell Offering: Writings by New England Mill Women*

(1840–1845), ed. Benita Eisler (Philadelphia: J.B. Lippincott, 1977), 150–54; hereafter cited parenthetically.

56. "Susan Miller," *The Lowell Offering: Writings by New England Mill Women (1840–1845)*, ed. Benita Eisler (Philadelphia: J.B. Lippincott, 1977), 172–82; hereafter cited parenthetically.

57. Cited in *The Factory Girls*, ed. Philip S. Foner (Urbana: University of Illinois Press, 1977), 61.

58. Gilman, "The Yellow Wallpaper," *Rediscoveries: American Short Stories by Women, 1832–1916*, ed. Barbara H. Solomon (New York: Penguin Books, 1994), 480–96.

59. Elizabeth Ammons, *Conflicting Stories: American Women Writers at the Turn into the Twentieth Century* (New York: Oxford University Press, 1991), 43.

60. Lanser, "Feminist Criticism, 'The Yellow Wallpaper,' and the Politics of Color in America," *Feminist Studies* 15 (1989): 424.

61. Ibid., 426.

62. Gilman, "The Yellow Wallpaper," 482.

63. Hill, *Charlotte Perkins Gilman: The Making of a Radical Feminist, 1860–1896* (Philadelphia: Temple University Press, 1980), 173.

64. Lanser, "Feminist Criticism," 425.

65. Gilman, "The Yellow Wallpaper," 489.

66. Gilman, "Old Mrs. Crosley," *Rediscoveries: American Short Stories by Women, 1832–1916*, ed. Barbara H. Solomon (New York: Penguin Books, 1994), 499.

67. Ibid., 501.

68. Ibid., 502.

69. Gilman, *Women and Economics: A Study of the Economic Relation Between Men and Women as a Factor in Social Evolution*, ed. Carl N. Degler (New York: Harper & Row, 1966), 255.

70. Ibid., 255–56.

71. Stowe, "The Seamstress," 110.

72. Sedgwick, "Fanny McDermot," *Rediscoveries: American Short Stories by Women, 1832–1916*, ed. Barbara H. Solomon (New York: Penguin Books, 1994), 113–54; hereafter cited parenthetically.

73. Fuller, *Woman in the Nineteenth Century*, 197.

74. Freedman, 514.

75. Woolf, "Women Novelists," *Contemporary Writers* (London: Hogarth Press, 1965), 26.

Works Cited

Ammons, Elizabeth. *Conflicting Stories: American Women Writers at the Turn into the Twentieth Century.* New York: Oxford University Press, 1991.

Anderson, Sherwood. "The Untold Lie." *Winesburg, Ohio.* New York: Penguin Books, 1976. 202–209.

"Ann and Myself: No Fiction." *The Lowell Offering: Writings by New England Mill Women (1840–1845),* ed. Benita Eisler. Philadelphia: J.B. Lippincott, 1977, 192–196.

Ashmore, Ruth. "The Intense Friendships of Girls." *Ladies Home Journal* 6 (July 1898): 20.

Auerbach, Nina. *Communities of Women: An Idea in Fiction.* Cambridge, Mass.: Harvard University Press, 1978.

Bates, H. E. "The Modern Short Story: Retrospect." *Short Story Theories,* ed. Charles E. May. Athens: Ohio University Press, 1976, 72–79.

Baym, Nina. "Melodramas of Beset Manhood: How Theories of American Fiction Exclude Women Authors." *American Quarterly* 33:2 (1981): 123–39.

Bernikow, Louise. *Among Women.* New York: Harmony Books, 1980.

Bowen, Susan Petigru King. "A Marriage of Persuasion." *Between Mothers and Daughters: Stories Across a Generation,* ed. Susan Koppelman. Old Westbury, N.Y.: The Feminist Press, 1985. 13–22.

Brown, Alice. "Joint Owners in Spain." *Women's Friendships: A Collection of Short Stories,* ed. Susan Koppelman. Norman: University of Oklahoma Press, 1991, 53–67.

———. "The Way of Peace." *Between Mothers and Daughters: Stories Across a Generation,* ed. Susan Koppelman. Old Westbury, N.Y.: The Feminist Press, 1985, 45–60.

Bruck, Peter. "Black American Short Fiction in the Twentieth Century: Problems of Audience, and the Evolution of Artistic Stances and Themes." *The Black American Short Story in the Twentieth Century: A Collection of Critical Essays,* ed. Peter Bruck. Amsterdam: B.R. Gruner Publishing Company, 1977, 1–19.

Cary, Alice. "Charlotte Ryan." *Clovernook Sketches and Other Stories,* ed. Judith Fetterley. New Brunswick, N.J.: Rutgers University Press, 1987, 105–37.

Child, Lydia Maria. "The Neighbour-in-Law." *Women's Friendships: A Collection of Short Stories,* ed. Susan Koppelman. Norman: University of Oklahoma Press, 1991, 6–15.

———. "The Quadroons." *Rediscoveries: American Short Stories by Women, 1832–1916,* ed. Barbara H. Solomon. New York: Penguin Books, 1994, 88–98.

———. "Slavery's Pleasant Homes—A Faithful Sketch." *The Heath Anthology of American Literature,* vol. 1, gen. ed. Paul Lauter. Lexington, Mass.: D.C. Heath, 1990, 1809–12.

Chodorow, Nancy. *The Reproduction of Mothering: Psychoanalysis and the Sociology of Gender.* Berkeley: University of California Press, 1978.

Chopin, Kate. "The Falling in Love of Fedora." *American Women Writers: Diverse Voices in Prose Since 1845,* eds. Eileen Barrett and Mary Cullinan. New York: St. Martin's Press, 1992, 145–47.

Christian, Barbara. *Black Women Novelists: The Development of a Tradition, 1892–1976.* Westport, Conn.: Greenwood Press, 1980.

Clinton, Catherine. *The Plantation Mistress: Woman's World in the Old South.* New York: Pantheon Books, 1982.

Cosslett, Tess. *Woman to Woman: Female Friendship in Victorian Fiction.* Brighton, Sussex: Harvest Press, 1988.

Cott, Nancy F. *The Bonds of Womanhood: "Woman's Sphere" in New England, 1780–1835.* New Haven: Yale University Press, 1977.

———. "Passionlessness: An Interpretation of Victorian Sexual Ideology, 1790–1850." *Signs* 4 (1978): 219–36.

Dally, Ann. *Inventing Motherhood: The Consequences of an Ideal.* London: Burnett Books, 1982.

Davidson, Cathy N. *Revolution and the Word: The Rise of the Novel in America.* New York: Oxford University Press, 1986.

Dobson, Joanne. "The American Renaissance Reenvisioned." *The (Other) American Traditions: Nineteenth-Century Women Writers,* ed. Joyce W. Warren. New Brunswick, N.J.: Rutgers University Press, 1993, 164–82.

Dublin, Thomas, ed. *Farm to Factory: Women's Letters, 1830–1860,* 2d ed. New York: Columbia University Press, 1993.

Eichenbaum, Luise, and Susie Orbach. *Between Women: Love, Envy, and Competition in Women's Friendships.* New York: Viking, 1988.

Eisler, Benita. "Introduction." *The Lowell Offering: Writings by New England Mill Women (1840–1845),* ed. Benita Eisler. Philadelphia: J.B. Lippincott, 1977, 9–41.

Evans, Sara M. *Born for Liberty: A History of Women in America.* New York: The Free Press, 1989.

Faderman, Lillian. "Lesbian Magazine Fiction in the Early Twentieth Century." *American Women Short Story Writers: A Collection of Critical Essays,* ed. Julie Brown. New York: Garland Publishing, 1995, 99–120.

———. *Surpassing the Love of Men: Romantic Friendship and Love Between Women from the Renaissance to the Present.* New York: William Morrow, 1981.

Fern, Fanny (Sara Willis Parton). "The Working-Girls of New York." *The Heath Anthology of American Literature,* 2d ed., vol. 1., gen. ed. Paul Lauter. Lexington, Mass.: D.C. Heath, 1990. 1955–1956.

Fetterley, Judith, and Marjorie Pryse. "Introduction." *American Women Regionalists, 1850–1910.* New York: W.W. Norton, 1992, xi–xx.

Fields, Annie, ed. *Letters of Sarah Orne Jewett.* Boston: Houghton Mifflin, 1911.

Finke, Laurie A. *Feminist Theory, Women's Writing.* Ithaca: Cornell University Press, 1992.

Fish, Stanley. *Is There a Text in This Class? The Authority of Interpretive Communities.* Cambridge, Mass.: Harvard University Press, 1980.

Foner, Philip S., ed. *The Factory Girls.* Urbana: University of Illinois Press, 1977.

Foster, Frances Smith. *Written by Herself: Literary Production by African American Women, 1746–1892.* Bloomington: Indiana University Press, 1993.

Fox-Genovese, Elizabeth. *Within the Plantation Household: Black and White Women of the Old South.* Chapel Hill: University of North Carolina Press, 1988.

Freedman, Estelle. "Separatism as Strategy: Female Institution Building and American Feminism, 1870–1930. *Feminist Studies* 5 (1979): 512–29.

Freeman, Mary E. Wilkins. "An Autobiography." *Critical Essays on Mary Wilkins Freeman,* ed. Shirley Marchalonis. Boston: G.K. Hall, 1991. 65–66.

———. "A Church Mouse." *A New England Nun and Other Stories.* New York: Harper & Brothers, 1891, 407–26.

———. "Friend of My Heart." *The Uncollected Stories of Mary Wilkins Freeman,* ed. Mary R. Reichardt. Jackson: University Press of Mississippi, 1992, 197–211.

———. "A Mistaken Charity." *Rediscoveries: American Short Stories by Women, 1832–1916,* ed. Barbara H. Solomon. New York: Penguin Books, 1994, 363–75.

———. "Old Woman Magoun." *The Heath Anthology of American Literature,* vol. 2, gen. ed. Paul Lauter. Lexington, Mass.: D.C. Heath, 1990, 159–71.

———. "On the Walpole Road." *American Women Regionalists, 1850–1910,* ed. Judith Fetterley and Marjorie Pryse. New York: W.W. Norton, 1992, 306–14.

———. "The Revolt of 'Mother'." *The Heath Anthology of American Literature,* vol. 2, gen. ed. Paul Lauter. Lexington, Mass.: D.C. Heath, 1990, 148–59.

———. "Sister Liddy." *A New England Nun and Other Stories.* New York: Harper & Brothers, 1891, 81–98.

Freud, Sigmund. "Female Sexuality." *Sigmund Freud, Collected Papers,* ed. James Strachey. London: Hogarth Press, 1956, 5:252–72.

Fuller, (Sarah) Margaret. [On Anna Barker]. Journal, October 1842. *The Essential Margaret Fuller,* ed. Jeffrey Steele. New Brunswick, N.J.: Rutgers University Press, 1992, 22–23.

———. *Summer on the Lakes: The Essential Margaret Fuller,* ed. Jeffrey Steele. New Brunswick, N.J.: Rutgers University Press, 1992, 69–225.

———. *Woman in the Nineteenth Century: The Essential Margaret Fuller,* ed. Jeffrey Steele. New Brunswick, N.J.: Rutgers University Press, 1992, 243–378.

Gardiner, Judith Kegan. "On Female Identity and Writing by Women." *Writing and Sexual Difference,* ed. Elizabeth Abel. Chicago: University of Chicago Press, 1982, 177–91.

Gilbert, Sandra M., and Susan Gubar. *The Madwoman in the Attic: The Woman Writer and the Nineteenth-Century Literary Imagination.* New Haven: Yale University Press, 1979.

Gilman, Charlotte Perkins. "Old Mrs. Crosley." *Rediscoveries: American Short Stories by Women, 1832–1916,* ed. Barbara H. Solomon. New York: Penguin Books, 1994, 496–504.

———. *Women and Economics: A Study of the Economic Relation Between Men and Women As a Factor in Social Evolution,* ed. Carl N. Degler. New York: Harper & Row, 1966.

———. "The Yellow Wallpaper." *Rediscoveries: American Short Stories by Women, 1832–1916,* ed. Barbara H. Solomon. New York: Penguin Books, 1994, 480–96.

Glaspell, Susan. "A Jury of Her Peers." *The Best Short Stories of 1917 and the Yearbook of the American Short Story,* ed. Edward J. O'Brien. Boston: Small, Mayourd and Company, 1918, 256–82.

Grimke, Sarah. *Letters on the Equality of the Sexes, and the Condition of Woman: Letters on the Equality of the Sexes and Other Essays,* ed. Elizabeth Ann Bartlett. New Haven: Yale University Press, 1988, 31–103.

Gullason, Thomas A. "What Makes a 'Great' Short Story Great?" *Studies in Short Fiction* 26:3 (1989): 267–77.

Hackleman, Leah. Preface to "Friends." By Edith Wharton. *Women's Friendships: A Collection of Short Stories,* ed. Susan Koppelman. Norman: University of Oklahoma Press, 1991. 68–72.

Hammer, Signe. *Daughters and Mothers: Mothers and Daughters.* New York: New York Times Book Company, 1975.

Hanson, Clare. "Introduction." *Re-reading the Short Story,* ed. Clare Hanson. London: Macmillan Press, 1989, 1–9.

———. "'Things Out of Words': Towards a Poetics of Short Fiction." *Re-Reading the Short Story,* ed. Clare Hanson. London: Macmillan Press, 1989, 22–33.

Hapke, Laura. *Tales of the Working Girl: Wage-Earning Women in American Literature, 1890–1925.* New York: Twayne Publishers, 1992.

Harper, Frances Ellen Watkins. "The Two Offers." *The Heath Anthology of American Literature,* vol. 1, 2d ed., gen. ed. Paul Lauter. Lexington, Mass.: D.C. Heath, 1994, 1973–80.

Harris, Susan K. "'But Is It Any Good?': Evaluating Nineteenth-Century American Women's Fiction." *American Literature* 63:1 (1991): 43–61.

Hill, Mary A. *Charlotte Perkins Gilman: The Making of a Radical Feminist, 1860–1896.* Philadelphia: Temple University Press, 1980.

Hobbs, Glenda. "Pure and Passionate: Female Friendship in Sarah Orne Jewett's 'Martha's Lady'." *Critical Essays on Sarah Orne Jewett,* ed. Gwen L. Nagel. Boston: G.K. Hall, 1984, 99–107.

Howells, William Dean. *The Rise of Silas Lapham.* New York: Signet Classics, 1963.

Hurst, Fannie. "Oats for the Woman." *Between Mothers and Daughters: Stories Across a Generation,* ed. Susan Koppelman. Old Westbury, N.Y.: The Feminist Press, 1985, 82–112.

Iser, Wolfgang. "Interaction Between Text and Reader." *The Reader in the Text: Essays on Audience and Interpretation,* ed. Susan R. Suleiman and Inge Crosman. Princeton: Princeton University Press, 1980, 106–19.

Jewett, Sarah Orne. "The Foreigner." *The World of Dunnet Landing: A Sarah Orne Jewett Collection,* ed. David Bonnell Green. Lincoln: University of Nebraska Press, 1962, 250–91.

———. "Martha's Lady." *Atlantic Monthly.* October 1897, 523–33.

———. "Miss Tempy's Watchers." *Women's Friendships: A Collection of Short Stories,* ed. Susan Koppelman. Norman: University of Oklahoma Press, 1991, 40–50.

———. "The Queen's Twin." *The World of Dunnet Landing: A Sarah Orne Jewett Collection,* ed. David Bonnell Green. Lincoln: University of Nebraska Press, 1962, 292–328.

Karcher, Carolyn L. Preface to "The Neighbour-in-Law." By Lydia Maria Child. *Women's Friendships: A Collection of Short Stories,* ed. Susan Koppelman. Norman: University of Oklahoma Press, 1991, 3–6.

Kerber, Linda K. "Woman's Place: The Rhetoric of Women's History." *Journal of American History* 75:1 (1981): 9–39.

Kessler, Carol Farley. Preface to "At Bay." By Elizabeth Stuart Phelps. *Women's Friendships: A Collection of Short Stories,* ed. Susan Koppelman. Norman: University of Oklahoma Press, 1991, 16–19.

King, Elizabeth Grace. "The Balcony." *American Women Regionalists, 1850–1910,* ed. Judith Fetterley and Marjorie Pryse. New York: W.W. Norton, 1995, 380–81.

———. "One of Us." *American Women Regionalists, 1850–1910,* ed. Judith Fetterley and Marjorie Pryse. New York: W.W. Norton, 1995, 390–94.

Kolodny, Annette. "Dancing Through the Minefield: Some Observations on the Theory, Practice and Politics of a Feminist Literary Criticism." *Feminist Studies* 6:1 (1980): 1–25.

———. "A Map for Rereading: Or, Gender and the Interpretation of Literary Texts." *New Literary History* 11:3 (1980): 451–67.

Koppelman, Susan. Afterword. *Women's Friendships: A Collection of Short Stories,* ed. Susan Koppelman. Norman: University of Oklahoma Press, 1991, 280–301.

———. Introduction. *Between Mothers and Daughters: Stories Across a Generation,* ed. Susan Koppelman. Old Westbury, N.Y.: The Feminist Press, 1985, xv–xxxix.

Lanser, Susan S. "Feminist Criticism, 'The Yellow Wallpaper,' and the Politics of Color in America." *Feminist Studies* 15 (1989): 415–41.

Lauter, Paul. "Is Frances Ellen Watkins Harper Good Enough to Teach?" *Legacy* 5 (1988): 27–32.

———. "Teaching Nineteenth-Century Women Writers." *The (Other) American Traditions: Nineteenth-Century Women Writers,* ed. Joyce W. Warren. New Brunswick, N.J.: Rutgers University Press, 1993, 280–301.

Leiby, James. *A History of Social Welfare and Social Work in the United States.* New York: Columbia University Press, 1978.

Levy, Helen Fiddyment. *Fiction of the Home Place: Jewett, Cather, Glasgow, Welty, and Naylor.* Jackson: University of Mississippi Press, 1992.

Lewis, Jan. "Mother's Love: The Construction of an Emotion in Nineteenth-Century America." *Social History and Issues in Human Consciousness: Some Interdisciplinary Connections,* ed. Andrew E. Barnes and Peter N. Stearns. New York: New York University Press, 1989, 209–29.

Martin, Robert K. "Knights-Errant and Gothic Seducers: The Representation of Male Friendship in Mid-Nineteenth-Century America." *Hidden from History: Reclaiming the Gay and Lesbian Past,* ed. Martin Bauml Duberman, Martha Vicinus, and George Chauncey, Jr. New York: NAL Books, 1989, 169–82.

Matthews, Brander. "The Philosophy of the Short-Story." *Short Story Theories,* ed. Charles E. May. Athens: Ohio University Press, 1976, 52–59.

McClave, Heather. Introduction. *Women Writers of the Short Story: A Collection of Critical Essays.* Englewood Cliffs, N.J.: Prentice-Hall, 1980, 1–10.

Melville, Herman. "The Paradise of Bachelors and the Tartarus of Maids." *Great Short Works of Herman Melville,* ed. Warner Berthoff. New York: Harper & Row, 1969, 202–22.

Miller, Jean Baker. *Toward a New Psychology of Women.* Boston: Beacon Press, 1976.

"The Patchwork Quilt." *The Lowell Offering: Writings by New England Mill Women (1840–1845),* ed. Benita Eisler. Philadelphia: J.B. Lippincott, 1977, 150–54.

Pattee, Fred Lewis. *The Development of the American Short Story: An Historical Survey.* New York: Bilbo and Pannen, 1966.

Phelps, Elizabeth Stuart. "The Angel Over the Right Shoulder." *Rediscoveries: American Short Stories by Women, 1832–1916,* ed. Barbara H. Solomon. New York: Penguin Books, 1994, 156–64.

———. "At Bay." *Women's Friendships: A Collection of Short Stories,* ed. Susan Koppelman. Norman: University of Oklahoma Press, 1991, 19–37.

————. "Old Mother Goose." *Between Mothers and Daughters: Stories Across a Generation*, ed. Susan Koppelman. Old Westbury, N.Y.: The Feminist Press, 1985, 23–41.

Poe, Edgar Allan. "The Cask of Amontillado." *Great Short Works of Edgar Allan Poe*, ed. G. R. Thompson. New York: Harper & Row, 1970, 496–503.

————. "The Philosophy of Composition." *Great Short Works of Edgar Allan Poe*, ed. G. R. Thompson. New York: Harper & Row, 1970, 528–42.

————. "Review of Twice-Told Tales by Nathaniel Hawthorne." *Great Short Works of Edgar Allan Poe*, ed. G. R. Thompson. New York: Harper & Row, 1970, 519–28.

Raymond, Janice G. *A Passion for Friends: Toward a Philosophy of Female Affection.* Boston: Beacon Press, 1986.

Reichardt, Mary R. *A Web of Relationship: Women in the Short Stories of Mary Wilkins Freeman.* Jackson: University Press of Mississippi, 1992.

Rich, Adrienne. "When We Dead Awaken: Writing as Re-Vision." *College English* 34:1 (1972): 18–30.

Ries, Adeline F. "Mammy: A Story." *The Unforgetting Heart: An Anthology of Short Stories by African American Women (1859–1993)*, ed. Asha Kanwar. San Francisco: Aunt Lute Books, 1993, 81–83.

Rohrberger, Mary. "The Short Story: A Proposed Definition." *Short Story Theories*, ed. Charles E. May. Athens: Ohio University Press, 1976, 80–82.

Romines, Ann. *The Home Plot: Women, Writing and Domestic Ritual.* Amherst: University of Massachusetts Press, 1992.

Rosenzweig, Linda W. *The Anchor of My Life: Middle-Class American Mothers and Daughters, 1880–1920.* New York: New York University Press, 1993.

Ryan, Mary P. *The Empire of the Mother: American Writing About Domesticity, 1830–1860,* in the series *Women and History*, numbers 2/3, ed. Eleanor S. Reimer. New York: Haworth Press, 1982.

————. "The Power of Women's Networks: A Case Study of Female Moral Reform in Antebellum America." *Feminist Studies* 5 (1979): 66–85.

————. *Womanhood in America: From Colonial Times to the Present*, 3d ed. New York: Franklin Watts, 1983.

Sahli, Nancy. "Smashing: Women's Relationships Before the Fall." *Chrysalis* 8 (1979): 17–27.

Schweickart, Patrocinio P. "Reading Ourselves: Toward a Feminist Theory of Reading." *Speaking of Gender*, ed. Elaine Showalter. New York: Routledge, 1989, 17–44.

Sedgwick, Catharine Maria. "Fanny McDermot." *Rediscoveries: American Short Stories by Women, 1832–1916*, ed. Barbara H. Solomon. New York: Penguin Books, 1994, 113–54.

Shinn, Thelma J. Preface to "Circumstance." By Harriet Prescott Spofford. *The Heath Anthology of American Literature*, vol. 2, gen. ed. Paul Lauter. Lexington, Mass.: D.C. Heath, 1990, 81–83.

Smith-Rosenberg, Carroll. "Beauty, the Beast and the Militant Woman: A Case Study in Sex Roles and Social Stress in Jacksonian America." *American Quarterly* 23 (1971): 562–84.

————. *Disorderly Conduct: Visions of Gender in Victorian America.* New York: Knopf, 1985.

————. "The Female World of Love and Ritual: Relations Between Women in Nineteenth-Century America." *Signs* 1 (1975): 1–29.

Spofford, Harriet Prescott. "Circumstance." *The Heath Anthology of American Literature,* vol. 2, gen. ed. Paul Lauter. Lexington, Mass.: D.C. Heath, 1990, 83–92.

Steele, Jeffrey. Introduction. *The Essential Margaret Fuller,* ed. Jeffrey Steele. New Brunswick, N.J.: Rutgers University Press, 1992, xi–xlix.

Stowe, Harriet Beecher. "The Seamstress." *Rediscoveries: American Short Stories by Women, 1832–1916,* ed. Barbara H. Solomon. New York: Penguin Books, 1994, 101–10.

———. *Uncle Tom's Cabin.* New York: New American Library, 1981.

"Susan Miller." *The Lowell Offering: Writings by New England Mill Women (1840–1845),* ed. Benita Eisler. Philadelphia: J.B. Lippincott, 1977, 172–82.

Theriot, Nancy M. *The Biosocial Construction of Femininity: Mothers and Daughters in Nineteenth-Century America.* New York: Greenwood Press, 1988.

Thompson, G. R. Introduction. *Great Short Works of Edgar Allan Poe,* ed. G. R. Thompson. New York: Harper & Row, 1970, 1–45.

Todd, Ruth D. "The Folly of Mildred: A Race Story with a Moral." *Short Fiction by Black Women, 1900–1920,* ed. Elizabeth Ammons. New York: Oxford University Press, 1991, 239–49.

Voss, Arthur. *The American Short Story: A Critical Survey.* Norman: University of Oklahoma Press, 1973.

Washington, Mary Helen. Introduction. *Invented Lives: Narratives of Black Women 1860–1960.* New York: Anchor Press, 1987, xv–xxxi.

Welter, Barbara. *Dimity Convictions: The American Woman in the Nineteenth Century.* Athens: Ohio University Press, 1976.

Wharton, Edith. "Friends." *Women's Friendships: A Collection of Short Stories,* ed. Susan Koppelman. Norman: University of Oklahoma Press, 1991, 72–91.

———. "The Quicksand." *The Collected Short Stories of Edith Wharton,* ed. R. W. B. Lewis. New York: Charles Scribner's Sons, 1968, 1:397–410.

Williams, Fannie Barrier. "After Many Days: A Christmas Story." *The Unforgetting Heart: An Anthology of Short Stories by African American Women (1859–1993),* ed. Asha Kanwar. San Francisco: Aunt Lute Books, 1993, 39–52.

Woloch, Nancy. *Women and the American Experience.* New York: Knopf, 1984.

Woolf, Virginia. "Women Novelists." *Contemporary Writers.* London: Hogarth Press, 1965, 24–27.

———. *A Room of One's Own.* New York: Harcourt Brace Jovanovich, 1929.

Yellin, Jean Fagan. "Lydia Maria Child, 1802–1880." *The Heath Anthology of American Literature,* vol. 1, gen. ed. Paul Lauter. Lexington, Mass.: D.C. Heath, 1990, 1,826–27.

Zagarell, Sandra A. "Narrative of Community: The Identification of a Genre." *Signs* 13 (1988): 498–527.

Zitkala-Sa. "The Trial Path." *American Women Regionalists, 1850–1910,* ed. Judith Fetterley and Marjorie Pryse. New York: W.W. Norton, 1992, 559–63.

Index